Dark Splendor

Dark Splendor

Spiritual Fitness for the Second Half of Life

Robert P. Vande Kappelle

RESOURCE *Publications* • Eugene, Oregon

DARK SPLENDOR
Spiritual Fitness for the Second Half of Life

Copyright © 2015 Robert P. Vande Kappelle. All rights reserved. Except for brief quotations in critical publications or reviews, no part of this book may be reproduced in any manner without prior written permission from the publisher. Write: Permissions. Wipf and Stock Publishers, 199 W. 8th Ave., Suite 3, Eugene, OR 97401.

Resource Publications
An Imprint of Wipf and Stock Publishers
199 W. 8th Ave., Suite 3
Eugene, OR 97401

www.wipfandstock.com

ISBN 13: 978-1-4982-3075-9

Manufactured in the U.S.A.   06/15/2015

Unless otherwise noted, Bible quotations are from the *New Revised Standard Version of the Bible*, copyright © 1989 by the Division of Christian Education of the National Council of the Churches of Christ in the United States of America. Used by permission.

To students in my Special Studies courses
in spirituality at Chautauqua Institution
(Chautauqua, New York)

If you bring forth what is within you, what you bring forth will save you. If you do not bring forth what is within you, what you do not bring forth will destroy you.

—GOSPEL OF THOMAS, 70

The greatest and most important problems of life are fundamentally unsolvable. They can never be solved, but only outgrown.

—CARL G. JUNG

I have an inner self of which I was ignorant. Everything goes thither now. What happens there I do not know.

—R. M. RILKE

Sin happens whenever we stop growing.

—ST. GREGORY OF NYSSA
(4TH CENTURY EASTERN CHRISTIAN THEOLOGIAN)

Contents

Preface | vii
Acknowledgments | xiv
Introduction | xv

Part I – Developing a Rule of Life

Chapter 1 – Models for Life's Journey | 3
Chapter 2 – Types of Spirituality | 23
Chapter 3 – Developing a Plan that Supports Spiritual Growth | 51

Part II – The First Half of Life

Chapter 4 – Essential Tasks for the Journey | 65
Chapter 5 – The Middle Passage (The Work of Midlife) | 76

Part III – The Second Half of Life

Chapter 6 – A Second Simplicity | 95
Chapter 7 – Regaining Soul | 101
Chapter 8 – Soulcraft | 108

Desiderata | 123

Appendix A – Qualities of the Second-Half Journey | 127
Appendix B – Practicing Presence: Helpful Methods | 129
Appendix C – Walking the Wire: A Sermon | 135

Bibliography | 141
Subject/Name Index | 145

Preface

> Midway this way of life we're bound upon,
> I woke to find myself in a dark wood,
> Where the right road was wholly lost and gone.
> —DANTE ALIGHIERI

A JOURNEY INTO "THE second half of life" awaits us all. This "further journey" is not chronological, nor does one magically stumble upon it at midlife or in times of crisis, though these often serve as catalysts. The second journey is largely unknown today, even by people we consider deeply religious, since most individuals and institutions remain stymied in the preoccupations of the first half of life, establishing identity, creating boundary markers, and seeking security. The first-half-of-life task, while essential, is not the full journey. Furthermore, one cannot walk the second journey with first-journey tools. One needs a new toolkit.

How can you know you are entering the second half of life? The following road markers are quite reliable: when you

- experience new urges
- sense a new vision
- are ready to let go of old securities
- are ready to risk giving up the patterns of the past for the promise of the future
- are as focused on the "inner" life as on the outer dimension of life.

While individuals can describe their experience of the second journey and even serve as mentors, they cannot define or outline the journey for others. This is due both to the uniqueness of the journey and to a subtle factor, known by generations of mystics and spiritual masters but elusive to many of our contemporaries: one does not choose this second journey; rather it chooses you. It finds you by means of your soul, your personal center and true home, the source of your true belonging. The soul comes to our aid through dreams, deep emotion, love, the quiet voice of guidance, synchronicities, revelations, hunches, and visions, and at times through illness, nightmares, and terrors. This is the identity that defines you, aligning you with your powers of nurturing, transforming, and creating, with your powers of presence and wonder. It is the soul that guides you, preparing the way and declaring you ready for this further journey.

If you haven't acquired conscious knowledge of your soul, you haven't yet learned of its power. To experience this power, which serves as a bridge to the second half of life, you must first get to know more thoroughly the place in life you already inhabit. This place consists of your relationships and roles in both society and nature. One achieves this knowledge and intimacy through the practice of mindfulness, learning to dwell deeply in the present moment.

This talk of the first and second half of life is not new. It has been embodied for centuries in the scriptures, tales, and experiences of men and women who found themselves on the further journey. At this point I must issue a disclaimer: I am not a psychiatrist, a counselor, a therapist, or a spiritual director, so if you are expecting advice or insight from a psychological professional or a mystical mentor, this book should not be at the top of your reading list. My training is in theology, particularly biblical theology, though my teaching, writing, and chaplaincy work have brought me some degree of competency in world religions, global cultures, and Christian spirituality.

This book has been incubating for a long time. During training for the Christian ministry I began to realize that without some direct experience of God, it was nearly useless for me to talk about religious reality to modern women and men. My quest continued with many ups and downs, but gradually I found a level path that kept me grounded through the highs and lows. It contained elements of three quite different approaches; the first was the writings of the masters of the devotional life; the second, the understanding of the psyche presented by depth psychology; and the third, my own religious practice. What became clear is that every religion has its origin in some primal encounter with the transcendent, as it presented to an

Preface

individual or to a tribe. Out of that encounter an image arose that bridged between the mystery and the perceiving consciousness. Over time, the ego tends to privilege its own constructs and confuse them with external reality, or confuse them with the mystery. Our finite sensibility cannot ultimately know infinite mystery. We have, however, an experience of transcendence, and call it by the name God. But what we call God is not the name or the image but the profound energy behind the image, which gives rise to the numinous encounter. What is experienced is our images of God, or the profundities of nature, or states of psychic transport, not the source from which they arise, the source that remains, in the words of theologian Karl Barth, "Wholly Other." The chasm that occurs between fundamentalism and atheism would be greatly reduced if this could be affirmed. Sadly, the quality of public discussion of spiritual matters has been so poor that great masses of modern humans have discarded what lies deepest within—their own religious yearning.

The pages that follow describe insights, disciplines, choices, and priorities that characterize "first-" and "second-half-of-life" experience, including wisdom I gained from teaching courses on spirituality at Washington & Jefferson College and to adults at Chautauqua Institution. I am deeply indebted to scholars who mentored me through theological and psychological writings, but also to generations of students who inspired me through journals, presentations, and class discussion, pressing me for clarity and always for truthfulness.

This book is not a method of study or a "cookie-cutter" approach to spirituality. In other words, you will not find here a set of rules for "being" more spiritual. In my estimation, spirituality doesn't work that way. Guidelines are helpful, and the experience of others can be beneficial, but ultimately it comes down to you, to your needs, experiences, and longings. It might be helpful to think of *Dark Splendor* as a window or mirror into your soul, which, like a thermometer or heart monitor, allows you to examine your current spiritual state, including the desires and experiences that led you to the present moment, and to determine further spiritual goals (based in part of the "longings" of your heart). Identifying those longings is part of the spiritual journey.

The subject of guiding and accompanying others on their spiritual journeys poses many problems. First of all, I must admit how little I know about this God of love who transforms us into citizens of the Kingdom of Love. Furthermore, having glimpsed light in the darkness, I confess to being in the shadow or in darkness much of the time. In addition, I am confronted with the inadequacy of my own spiritual life, finding within cowardice and fear, anger and lack of compassion, selfishness and pride, ignorance and confusion. At times I am confronted with the presence of evil, both within me and around me, which threatens to destroy my hope, joy, and equanimity. And then at times I am again in the great wilderness of doubt. Thankfully, these very experiences of inadequacy often force us back to the journey and to our spiritual home.

Wisdom traditions worldwide say there is no greater blessing than to live the life of your soul, the source of deepest personal fulfillment and of greatest service to others. The soul is the locus of authentic personal power—not power over people and things, but rather of partnership with others, the power to co-create life and to cooperate with an evolving universe.

Psychologists and religious mystics agree: life is simultaneously dark and bright, sad and joyous, pessimistic and optimistic, a mixture of physical pain, emotional suffering, mental euphoria, and spiritual consolation. Sentient life begins in darkness, and then emerges into light. Birth, infancy, indeed the period of one's youth, is often described as light, for it is a generally joyous, hopeful, and optimistic time of life. During maturity and the onset of old age, the pendulum swings, since this period often brings diminished mental and physical capacities. While darkness is certainly present in the latter years of one's life—perhaps more than before—some older folks experience a surprising transformative perspective. For them "the light shines in the darkness, and the darkness [does] not overcome it." We envy their attitude, their courage, and their vision, an experience John of the Cross called "luminous darkness," Richard Rohr "bright sadness," and which I describe as "dark splendor." Such people are experiencing "the second half of life."

Overview

Readers interested primarily in the topics of the first and second journeys of life may consider reading chapters 1 and 2 selectively or simply treat them as reference material, since they contain technical material on spirituality and personality theory. Chapter 1 surveys psychological developmental models as rationales for thinking and living progressively. Chapter 2 examines the relationship between personality and spirituality, focusing

Preface

on the contributions of Swiss psychiatrist Carl G. Jung and on Jungian personality type theory.

Chapter 3 encourages readers to construct a realistic rule of life, a plan to enhance their spiritual growth and thereby deepen their experience with the divine. Chapter 4 introduces the tasks of the-first-half-of life journey, underscoring the symbiotic relationship between law and freedom. Readers are introduced to the "loyal soldier," a vital figure during this phase, but whose role diminishes with time. Chapter 5 discusses the "midlife" transition, including its psychological and spiritual importance as a rite of passage for the second-half journey. Chapter 6 introduces the second-half-of-life journey, identifying seven transformational qualities that characterize this "second simplicity." Chapter 7 discusses the four landscapes or levels of selfhood—body, mind, soul, and spirit—and their interrelationship. Chapter 8 discusses five qualities—simplicity, stillness, study, stamina, and service—and how together they shape the second-half-of-life spirituality. When these five pathways converge in soulfulness, they result in enhanced service to God and to humanity.

Acknowledgements

THIS BOOK REPRESENT EXTENSIONS of thought that appear in earlier volumes, particularly *Love Never Fails, The Invisible Mountain, Into Thin Places, Beyond Belief,* and *Iron Sharpens Iron,* in addition to my biblical commentaries *Hope Revealed, Truth Revealed,* and *Wisdom Revealed.*

I acknowledge particular indebtedness to Richard Foster, Matthew Fox, Thich Nhat Hanh, James Hollis, Elizabeth Lesser, Susan Annette Muto, Bill Plotkin, and Richard Rohr.[1] Plotkin's insights as a spiritual guide, particularly his groundbreaking Wheel of Life model in *Nature and the Human Soul: Cultivating Wholeness and Community in a Fragmented World,* is truly inspirational and transformative. Of the many mentors in my spiritual journey, none have impacted me more profoundly than Richard Rohr. *Falling Upward: A Spirituality for the Two Halves of Life,* destined to be a classic, demonstrates how human failings can be the foundation for ongoing spiritual growth.

This book could not have been written without the ongoing encouragement and support of my wife Susan, who daily models what it means to be a "Jesus person." She introduced me to the writings of Richard Rohr, whose book *Falling Upward* familiarized me with the second-half-of-life journey. I am particularly grateful for the friendship and support of David Novitsky, Olga Solovieva, Dan Stinson, and Walt Weaver, colleagues at Washington & Jefferson College. I dedicate this book to students in my Special Studies courses in spirituality at Chautauqua Institution (Chautauqua, New York), for thirty years the crucible of my spiritual, intellectual, and aesthetic transformation.

---

1. Their works are listed in the bibliography.

Introduction

One cannot live the afternoon of life according to the program of life's morning; for what was great in the morning will be of little importance in the evening, and what in the morning was true will at evening have become a lie.

—CARL G. JUNG

THERE IS MUCH EVIDENCE that suggests that there are at least two major tasks to human life. The first task is to build a strong "container" or identity; the second is to find the contents that the container is meant to hold.[1] The first task is obvious, one we take for granted as the purpose of life: surviving successfully. Many cultures across history, most empires in antiquity, and the majority of individuals in the modern period have focused on first-half-of-life tasks, because of a lack of vision, and because it is all they have time for. We all want to complete successfully the task that life first hands us: establishing an identity, a home, a career, relationships, friends, community, and security, all foundational for getting started in life.

Most of us are never told that we can set out from the known and the familiar to take on a further journey. Our institutions, including our churches, are almost entirely configured to encourage, support, reward, and validate the tasks of the first half of life. Shocking and disappointing as it may be, we are more struggling to survive than to thrive, more focused on "getting through" or trying to get to the top than finding out what is really at the top or was already at the bottom. As wilderness guide Bill Plotkin puts it, many of us learn to do our "survival dance," but we never get to our actual "sacred dance."

---

1. Rohr, *Falling Upward*, xiii.

Introduction

Perhaps this is the symbolic meaning of Moses breaking the first tablets of the law, only to go back up the mountain and have them redone by Yahweh (Exod. 32:19–35). The second set of tablets emerged after a face-to-face encounter with God, which changes everything. Our first understanding of law must fail us and disappoint us. Only after breaking the first tablets of the law is Moses a real leader and prophet. Only afterward does he see God's glory (Exod. 33:18–19), and only afterward does his face "shine" (Exod. 34:29–30). It might just be the difference between the two halves of life. As Richard Rohr states it, "we grow spiritually much more by doing something wrong than by doing it right." The Dalai Lama said much the same thing: "Learn and obey the rules very well, so you will know how to break them properly." All the world's religions at the mature levels say the same thing. In the beginning, we tend to think that God really cares about postures in worship, sacred times and places, and the wording of our prayers. Once we reach the level of constant communion, when we discover the God of unconditional love, we discover that the techniques, formulas, sacraments, and rituals are just a dress rehearsal for the real thing, a conscious and loving existence. This is the highest form of worship and praise.

When we speak of the second half of life, we are not thinking in a strictly chronological way. Some young people, especially those who have experienced early suffering, trauma, or life-altering events, may already be there, and some older folks will never reach it. Women, generally more nurturing and compassionate than men and less competitive and violent by nature, are naturally inclined to this reality, though many are prevented, either by duty, obligation, or opportunity, from engaging fully with it.

It takes most of us a long time to discover "the task within the task," as Richard Rohr calls us, a deeper meaning or purpose underlying one's activities or motivation. It is when we begin to pay attention, and seek integrity precisely in "the task within the task," that we begin to move from the first to the second half of our own lives.

James Hollis, in *Finding Meaning in the Second Half of Life*, writes: "For all the changes that have occurred over the last four centuries, perhaps our greatest loss is the diminution of dialogue about that mystery toward which the word soul is meant to point."[2] In that book he poses questions that we need to ask in order for inner growth to occur, for the healing of the soul to take place. The questions, in modified form, are:

---

2. Hollis, *Second Half of Life*, 237.

Introduction

1. What has brought you to this place in your journey, this moment in your life?
2. What gods, forces, family, and social environment have framed your reality, whether supporting or constricting it?
3. Why, even when things are going well, do things not feel quite right?
4. Why in life does so much seem a disappointment, a betrayal, a bankruptcy of expectations?
5. Why do you believe that you have so much to hide from others, from yourself?
6. Why does life seem a script written elsewhere, and you barely consulted, if at all?
7. Why have you come to this book, or why has it come to you, now?
8. Why does the idea of the soul both trouble you and feel familiar?
9. Is the life you are living too small for your soul's desire?

While all the questions may not apply, I recommend that you reread each question carefully, taking time to write answers to those that seem relevant at this time.

Start recording your dreams, and seek help with their interpretation. Hollis speaks of a man who had spent his life in academia, brilliantly serving the life of the mind. Now retired, he fell into a depression, for he had no structure to carry his psychological energies, no insistent agenda of values to serve, no sense of who he was apart from his role. One day, driving home after an hour of therapy, he began to weep uncontrollably and unexplainably. That night he dreamed that he was back in the university setting, sitting for an exam for which he was unprepared. All of a sudden he realized he didn't have to take this course. Relieved, he tore up the blue book and walked out of the room. Upon awakening he found himself ready to begin anew, living a different life—his life.

Hollis recalls the first dream he had in Switzerland, during midlife, when he was studying to become a Jungian therapist. He dreamed he was a knight upon the ramparts of a medieval castle with arrows flying all about. At the forest's edge he saw a witchlike figure who was directing the assault. He felt great anxiety, fearing the castle would fall, and at the end of the dream the castle's fate was very much in doubt. His analyst suggested that he lower the drawbridge of his castle and go out and meet the witch.

Introduction

Naturally, he feared such an encounter, but he trusted his analyst's advice, recognizing that he was at the beginning of a long journey through a dark wood, a wood in which he had lived for many years, before it had come to consciousness.[3]

Recently I dreamt I was a teenager at an unknown location and in need of a ride home. I saw my father heading toward a car and asked if he would give me a ride.[4] The ride never occurred, however, for my father disappeared. I went looking for him and found him examining rings with a jeweler. The jewels seemed small in size, but exquisite. I moved on and eventually found myself seated at a large table in a conference room, surrounded by offices. The tabletop doubled as a piano. There were no keys, only the tabletop, but as I began playing on the table, I instinctively knew where to find the proper notes for an advanced rendition of the hymn "Open My Eyes, That I May See." People gathered around the table, listening to my performance. Finally, a man dashed through the room, gave me an angry look, and entered his office, slamming the door. I recognized him as the executive director of the organization.

Later, as I pondered the dream and its meaning, I gained valuable insight into my decision to retire. My longing for home represents the residential ego structure, the false self whose values and scenario desire to govern one's choices. Apparently I longed to return to the past, but the past was no longer viable, for new values require a new self.

The table in my dream contained a hidden keyboard, which I was able to play. When I shared the dream with my wife, a pastoral therapist, she encouraged me to "*be* the table," meaning that from her perspective, every part of a dream is important because of what it tells us about ourselves. The meaning of being the table is that in my retirement I continue to have utilitarian value, a setting where business is conducted and decisions are made. Moreover, as pianist and piano, I can both play and be played during retirement. The dream indicates that I am becoming more adept at finding inner notes, notes that cannot be seen, translating them into beneficial "music."

---

3. Ibid., 1–3. In analyzing his dream, Hollis notes that the knight represents ego consciousness and the witch the split-off parts of his feeling life. Beyond them both is the Self, the architect of the dream, which summons consciousness and asks greater accountability of it.

4. Readers should know that at the time of my dream, my father had been deceased for fifteen years. As a youngster he had lost his right eye in a sledding accident. Though he drove cars during his early adulthood, I can never recall his having done so during my lifetime.

Introduction

Another interpretation is that my father, legally blind, has recovered his sight, and that I, fully sighted, have become wounded in a way that, while diminishing my physical sight, enhances my spiritual vision, enabling me to improvise.[5] Now, when I play music (when I act and exist), I am able to walk "by faith" as well as "by sight," bringing forth music from my inner self (my True Self within the table) that formerly emanated primarily from my external self. The words of the hymn that I played: "Open my eyes that I may see, glimpses of truth Thou hast for me; place in my hands the wonderful key, that shall unclasp and set me free," seem particularly meaningful in my post-operative condition, while also addressing my current spiritual state.

At the end of the dream an authority figure storms through the conference room, annoyed and aloof in his anger, but no one pays attention. His presence is fleeting and his impact upon others minimal. Perhaps his anger stems from this realization. Am I that authority figure? Does this person represent my former role as authoritative teacher/minister, a role now fleeting, its influence vanishing behind closed opportunities? If so, this is a hopeful sign, for in retirement I find that authority figures no longer intimidate me.

What these dreams have in common is the overthrow of the ego's understanding of self and world and an invitation by the soul to live more consciously in the second half of life. But first comes the confounding of consciousness, and the sense that one has been pulled from a familiar environment into some darker wood.

Every night we dream, and every day the world is full of clues as to the will of the soul, if we are willing or desperate enough to pay attention. If and when we begin to take this inner life seriously, our psychic gravity begins to change. From this internal transformation, profound changes of the outer world become possible.

When you have finished the first list of questions, take time to address the following list, deeper, more difficult, and certainly more personal than the first list. Consider recording your answers in a journal.

---

5. Several months after the start of my retirement I was diagnosed with an ocular melanoma, a rare cancerous tumor in my left eye. My physician recommended a form of radiation treatment known as brachytherapy, whereby a small shield encasing radioactive seeds is attached to the outside surface of the eye for four days. At the end I could see again, though the vision in my left eye took several months before it returned to normal. A CT Scan confirmed there was no metastasis. The tumor was shrinking in size, absorbed by the body; I was becoming cancer free.

Introduction

1. Where has life, in its unfairness, fixated you, causing you to return to this wounding as a provisional definition and limitation of your possibilities? Do you serve this wound, or can you serve something larger, which serves you in return?
2. Where has life blessed you? What have you done with that gift? How have you accepted the responsibility that goes with it?
3. Where are you blocked by fear, stuck, rigid, resistant to change?
4. What is the fear beneath the fear, the fear that intimidates you, the fear from your past that causes you to ignore the empowered adult you have since become?
5. Where was your father stuck, and where has that stuck place shown up in your life? Where was your mother stuck, and where has that stuck place shown up in your life? Are you repeating your parents' patterns, or treating the problem in ways that bring harm and further self-alienation? What legacy will you pass on to your children?
6. Where do you avoid conflict, the necessary conflict of values, and therefore avoid living in fidelity with who you are?
7. What ideas, habits, or behavioral patterns are holding you back from the larger journey of the soul?
8. Where are you still looking for permission to live your life? Are you waiting for someone else to write the script of your life for you?
9. Where do you need to grow up? When will this happen? Can someone else do it for you?
10. What have you always felt called toward, but feared to do?
11. Why is now the time, if ever it is to happen, for you to answer the summons of the soul, to live the second, larger life?[6]

Like individuality, each person has a spirituality native to his or her own personality. Like personality, spirituality also yearns for growth and expression. One's spirituality, like one's personality, can never be determined by someone else. It can be influenced by others, as in the case of parents and other authority figures, but ultimately the choice of spirituality must be one's own.

---

6. Hollis, *Second Half of Life*, 235–260.

Introduction

Dark Splendor is grounded in the conviction that humans have the capacity to transcend conventional spirituality to a genuine and wholesome faith that is dynamic rather than static, future-oriented rather than past-oriented, and affirmed rather than passively acquired. This capacity is fueled by three principles:

1. that life is more important than death – this principle encourages us to pursue life-enhancing opportunities;

2. that whatever does not grow dies – this principle encourages us to remain open to change and newness;

3. that all truth is God's truth – this principle encourages us to remain open to truth wherever it may be found and wherever it leads.

Part I – Developing a "Rule of Life"

CHAPTER 1

Models for Life's Journey

> Beyond rational and critical
> thinking, we need to be called again.
> This can lead to the discovery
> of a "second naiveté," which is
> a return to the joy of our first
> naiveté, but now totally new,
> inclusive, and mature thinking.
>
> —PAUL RICOEUR

MOST HUMANS, ANCIENT AND modern alike, pattern their lives after some model, whether consciously or unconsciously. These models can be cultural, civic, intellectual, historical, cyclical, developmental, religious, or spiritual. Many people follow more than one pattern simultaneously. Most educated people in the West today have little trouble identifying with terms such as premodern, modern, or postmodern. They are also familiar with Karl Marx's adaptation of Hegel's thesis, antithesis, and synthesis as stages of social and economic development. This model has also been used to describe three stages of growth toward citizenship: claiming (thesis), doubting (antithesis), and redeeming (synthesis). A similar pattern can be observed in the development of biblical wisdom thought, from the conventional wisdom and values found in the book or Proverbs (thesis), to the unconventional or counter-order wisdom found in the books of Ecclesiastes and Job, where God seems distant, life disorderly and unfair, and where we find skeptical approaches to life (antithesis), to the later synthesis in the intertestamental books of Sirach (Ecclesiasticus) and Wisdom of Solomon, which blend traditional Jewish religious notions with progressive Hellenistic philosophical

Part I – Developing a "Rule of Life"

approaches. This synthesis produced new possibilities for Jews and later for Christians, including belief in the resurrection of the body and eternal life in heaven and hell. This synthesis also helped Roman Christians conceptualize doctrines such as the deity of Christ and the Trinity.

A similar model, consisting of precritical, critical, and postcritical stages, has been applied to theological, existential, and intellectual development. The first phase, also called precritical naiveté, first naiveté, or first simplicity, is an early state in which children accept whatever significant authority figures in their lives tell them to be true as indeed true. For some this state is short-lived; for others, it can last a lifetime. In their early teens, some begin to question their beliefs, experiencing a collision between childhood beliefs and those of modernity. In late adolescence college students often become exposed to the scholarly study of religion, to teachings of religions different from their own, to claims of science, and to atheistic or agnostic professors and points of view. Those who take these views seriously often enter the stage of critical understanding, from which there seems to be no way back. Some remain perplexed about God and conclude that there probably is no such reality. Those who persevere in their faith journey often discover that agnosticism and atheism are more like temporary stops than final destinations. Something happens to them—a mystical experience, something traumatic, a relationship, a sudden realization—and the word "God" becomes meaningful once again, only this time not as a reference to a supernatural being "out there" but to the sacred at the center of existence. God is no longer a mere idea or an article of belief external to oneself but rather an element of experience. Such persons have reached the state of postcritical understanding (also called postcritical naiveté, second naiveté, or second simplicity), a state where one participates in religious rituals because they are meaningful and not because they are required, where one hears ancient biblical stories as "true" while knowing them as not literally true.

In antiquity, people living in traditional or nature-based societies generally thought of life as revolving around the seasons, passing naturally from spring to summer, autumn, and winter. Each season, it seems, also had a connection to a compass point (east=spring; south=summer; west=autumn; north=winter). In addition, people were guided by the four times of day (sunrise, midday, sunset, and midnight). Over time, various models of spirituality came to be based on the seasons of nature, such as Brian McLaren's four-stage framework: Simplicity (the Springlike Season of Spiritual Awakening), Complexity (the Summerlike Season of Spiritual Strengthening), Perplexity (The Autumnlike Season of Spiritual Surviving), and Harmony (the Winterlike Season of Spiritual Deepening).[1] Wisely, McLaren acknowledges that unpredictability and surprise are also inherent in the simple framework of four seasons in the spiritual life, and that we should not be lulled into false security by the metaphor of predictable patterns of the seasons. The point is not to stay in one season forever, nor to get to another season as soon as possible. Rather, the point is to live each stage well, to learn what each day and season has to teach, and to live and enjoy life fully in each of its seasons.

Similarly, though not overtly so, Matthew Fox develops a fourfold understanding of the spiritual journey that he labels (1) Via Positiva (Befriending Nature); (2) Via Negativa (Befriending Darkness); (3) Via Creative (Befriending Creativity); and (4) Via Transformativa (Befriending New Creation).[2] Deeply influenced by nature and its original goodness, his groundbreaking book *Original Blessing* describes many of the qualities and perspectives of "second-half-of-life living" without using the term.

A Classic Hindu Model

Ancient Hindu teaching established a threefold pattern for life found in many human cultures across the globe, both ancient and modern. The first stage is that of *the student*. Traditionally this stage began after the rite of initiation, between the ages of eight and twelve, and lasted for twelve years. Life's prime responsibility at this stage was to learn, to offer a receptive mind to all that one's teacher(s) could transmit from the past. What was to be learned included factual information, but much more, for India had little interest in knowledge for knowledge's sake. Habits were to be cultivated and character formed. The entire training was more like an apprenticeship in which information "became incarnated in skill."[3]

The second stage, beginning with marriage, was that of *the householder*, during which period one's interests and energies naturally turn outward, focusing on family, vocation, and community. The role of householder and provider was significant in that it was viewed as the cornerstone of society.

---

1. McLaren, *Naked Spirituality*, 26–27.
2. Fox, *Original Blessing*.
3. Smith, *World's Religions*, 51.

Part I – Developing a "Rule of Life"

The third stage was that of *retirement*, when individuals could take advantage of the license of age and withdraw from the social obligations of life's previous stages. Thus far society had required the individual to specialize, but the time had come to begin "one's true adult education, to discover who one is and what life is about."[4] Based on the notion of reincarnation, Hindu society recognized that this was the time to prepare for one's rebirth in the life to come after death.

A fourth stage, open to members of the upper classes at any time, though often entered at or after retirement, consists of an ascetic stage when one becomes a homeless *sannyasin*, defined in the ancient scriptures as "one who neither hates nor loves anything." Far from wanting to "be somebody," the *sannyasin* wished to remain a nonperson on the surface in order to be joined to all at the root. According to the Hindu texts, the *sannyasin* "lives identified with the eternal self and beholds nothing else." Such persons, taking no thought of the future and looking with indifference upon the present, are at rest in the presence of God, the essence of bliss.

John Wesley's "Trilateral" Model

Another model for life, more modern than the Hindu, does not divide life into three (or four) stages, but rather presents an ideal way of living that focuses on attitudes toward wealth and on the use of one's resources. This approach is based on the life of John Wesley (1703–1791), the founder of the Protestant denomination known as Methodism. Called Wesley's "Trilateral," the model promotes the following ideals: "Gain all you can; save all you can; give all you can." Wesley believed that when it came to economics, Christians should be industrious and clever, working hard and long in order to gain all they could. Wesley followed his advice, becoming one of the highest earning preachers of all times. Based on current dollar amounts, he earned the equivalent of $1.4 million in a single year. Despite his entrepreneurial spirit, Wesley cautioned that money should never be illegally gained, and never at the expense of one's health or by taking advantage of others. Given these cautions on wrongful gain, Wesley encouraged Christians to be thrifty and industrious not in order to hoard their money but in order to be generous.

His second concept was about saving. What he meant by this was not that one should squirrel as much as possible into saving accounts, but rather

4. Ibid., 53.

that one should be frugal, careful in spending. Rather than squandering money on extravagance and sensual living, Wesley called for simplicity and plainness. His third concept was about giving: give all you can. This was the motivation of his entire view of life, including personal economics. The trilateral stands on giving: one gains and saves in order to give. How should one give, and to whom? Generosity begins with oneself, meeting basic needs. Then one gives to family and employees what is their fair share. Third, one gives to other Christians, beginning with one's home church. Finally, one gives to all in need, even if they are not believers.

Wesley practiced what he preached. In the year he earned the equivalent of $1.4 million, he lived on 2 percent of his income and gave 98 percent of it away. During his lifetime he earned the equivalent of $30 million, but when he died he left only a few miscellaneous coins and a couple of silver spoons. He had given away all the rest. What a way to die . . . and live!

Psychological Developmental Models

There is in every human an impetus which, when nourished, seeks health and wholeness. Having examined cultural patterns for life, including India's stages of life and Wesley's way of life for believers who wished to model Christian discipleship, we need to consider psychological and spiritual developmental models. Healthy human beings are said to go through discernible stages of growth throughout their lifetime.

1. Erik Erikson's Psychosocial Developmental Model

According to psychologist Erik Erikson (1902–1994), psychosocial development proceeds by critical steps, described as infancy (birth to 18 months), early childhood (2 to 3 years of age), preschool (3 to 5 years), school age (6 to 11 years), adolescence (12 to 18 years), young adulthood (19 to 40 years), middle adulthood (40 to 65 years), and maturity (65 to death). Each stage is marked by crisis, connoting not a catastrophe but a turning point, a crucial period of increased vulnerability and heightened potential. At such points achievements are won or failures occur, leaving the future to some degree better or worse but in any case, restructured. For each stage Erikson defined a basic conflict, important events, and outcomes, as the following chart indicates.

Part I – Developing a "Rule of Life"

Stage	Basic Conflict	Important Event	Outcome
Infancy	Trust vs. Mistrust	Feeding	Children develop a sense of trust or mistrust based on whether caregivers provide reliable care and affection.
Early Childhood	Autonomy vs. Shame and Doubt	Toilet Training	Children need to develop a sense of personal control over physical skills and a sense of independence. While success leads to feelings of autonomy, failure results in feelings of shame and doubt.
Preschool	Initiative vs. Guilt	Exploration	Children need to begin asserting control and power over their environment. Success leads children to a sense of purpose. Children who exert too much power experience disapproval, resulting in a sense of guilt.

Stage	Basic Conflict	Important Event	Outcome
School Age	Industry vs. Inferiority	School	Children need to cope with new social and academic demands. Success leads to a sense of competence, while failure results in feelings of inferiority.
Adolescence	Identity vs. Role Confusion	Social Relationships	Teens need to develop a sense of self and personal identity. Success leads to an ability to stay true to oneself, while failure leads to role confusion and a weak sense of self.
Young Adulthood	Intimacy vs. Isolation	Relationships	Young adults need to form intimate, loving relationships with other people. Success leads to strong relationships, while failure results in loneliness and isolation.

Part I – Developing a "Rule of Life"

Stage	Basic Conflict	Important Event	Outcome
Middle Adulthood	Generativity vs. Stagnation	Work and Parenthood	Adults need to create or nurture things that will outlast them, often by having children or creating a positive change that benefits other people. Success leads to feelings of usefulness and accomplishment, while failure results in shallow involvement in the world.
Maturity	Ego Integrity vs. Despair	Reflection on Life	Older adults need to look back on life and feel a sense of fulfillment. Success at this stage leads to feelings of wisdom, while failure results in regret, bitterness, and despair.

The strength acquired at one stage is tested by the necessity to transcend it, meaning that the individual is able to take chances in the next stage with what was most vulnerably precious in the previous one. For example, healthy children will not fear life if their elders have integrity enough not to fear death.

2. Jean Piaget's Theory of Cognitive Development

Swiss developmental psychologist Jean Piaget (1896–1980) was known for his theory of cognitive development in children. A pioneer in his field, his ideas were not widely known until the 1960s. Piaget believed that the process of thinking and intellectual development of children should be regarded as an extension of the biological process of evolutionary adaptation. He argued that human intelligence develops in a series of stages that are related to age and are progressive because one stage must be accomplished before the next can occur. His contributions led to the emergence of the study of development as a major discipline within psychology.

Piaget's stages of cognitive development focus on infancy through young adulthood and are based on four eras as follows:

Sensorimotor Stage (0 to 2 years)

During this first stage, children learn entirely through the movements they make and the sensations that result. They learn:

- that they exist separately from the objects and people around them
- that they can cause things to happen, and
- that things continue to exist even when they can't see them.

Preoperational Stage (2 to 7 years)

Once children acquire language, they are able to use symbols (such as words or pictures) to represent objects. Their thinking is still egocentric, for they assume that everyone else sees things from the same viewpoint as they do. They are able to understand concepts like counting, classifying according to similarity, and past-present-future, but generally they are still focused primarily on the present and on the concrete rather than the abstract.

Concrete Operational Stage (7 to 11 years)

At this stage, children are able to see things from different points of view and to imagine events that occur outside their own lives. Some organized, logical thought processes are now evident and children are able to:]

- order objects by size, color gradient, etc.
- understand that if $3 + 4 = 7$ then $7 - 4 = 3$
- understand that a red square can belong to both "red" and "square" categories
- understand that a short wide cup can hold the same amount of liquid as a tall thin cup
- However, thinking still tends to be tied to concrete reality.

Part I – Developing a "Rule of Life"

Formal Operational Stage (11 to adulthood)

Around the onset of puberty, children are able to reason in much more abstract ways and to test hypotheses using systematic logic. There is a much greater focus on possibilities and on ideological issues.

3. Lawrence Kohlberg's Theory of Moral Development

A third developmental model is that of Lawrence Kohlberg (1927–1987), an American psychologist best known for his theory of stages of moral development. He delineates six stages of development, from pre-conventional to post-conventional morality as follows:

Pre-Conventional Morality

Stage 1: Obedience or Punishment Orientation

This is the stage that all young children start at (and a few adults remain in). Rules are seen as being fixed and absolute. Obeying the rules is important because it means avoiding punishment

Stage 2: Self-Interest Orientation

As children grow older, they begin to see that other people have their own goal and preferences and that often there is room for negotiation. Decisions are made based on the principle of "What's in it for me?" For example, an older child might reason: "If I do what mom or dad wants me to do, they will reward me. Therefore I will do it."

Conventional Morality

Stage 3: Social Conformity Orientation

By adolescence, most individuals have developed to this stage. There is a sense of what "good boys" and "nice girls" do and the emphasis is on living up to social expectations and norms because of how they impact day-to-day relationships.

Stage 4: Law and Order Orientation

By the time individuals reach adulthood, they usually consider society as a whole when making judgments. The focus is on maintaining law and order by following the rules, doing one's duty and respecting authority.

Post-Conventional Morality

Stage 5: Social Contract Orientation

At this stage, people understand that there are differing opinions out there on what is right and wrong and that laws are really just a social contract based on majority decision and inevitable compromise. People at this stage sometimes disobey rules if they find them to be inconsistent with their personal values and will also argue for certain laws to be changed if they are no longer "working." Our modern democracies are based on the reasoning of Stage 5.

Stage 6: Universal Ethics Orientation

Few people operate at this stage all the time. It is based on abstract reasoning and the ability to put oneself in other people's shoes. At this stage, people have a principled conscience and will follow universal ethical principles regardless of what the official laws and rules are.

4. James Fowler's Stages of Faith

As humans grow by progressing physically, psychologically, emotionally, and even intellectually, so they undergo various stages of growth in their faith. Out of one's individuality flows a spirituality that also yearns for growth and expression. What Erikson contributed to our understanding of the stages of psychosocial development, Jean Piaget to the stages of cognitive development, and Lawrence Kohlberg to the stages of moral development, so James Fowler (b. 1940) did for spirituality in developing seven stages of faith, from stage zero, called "primal faith," when infants and toddlers develop (or fail to develop) a sense of safety about the universe and the divine, to a sixth stage called "universalizing faith," a rarely reached stage of those who live their lives to the full in service of others without any real fears or worries. Most people plateau at what Fowler calls the "synthetic-conventional" stage, one arising in adolescence. At this stage authority is usually placed in individuals or groups that represent one's beliefs.

Fowler's stages of faith are listed below, followed by M. Scott Peck's simplified version:

Stage 0: Primal Faith (0 to 2 years): This stage is characterized by early learning the safety of the environment. Under consistent nurture, children develop a sense of safety about the universe and the divine. Negative experiences (neglect and abuse) lead to distrust of the universe and the divine.

Part I – Developing a "Rule of Life"

Stage 1: Intuitive-Projective (3 to 7 years): This is the stage of preschool children in which fantasy and reality often are mixed together. However, during this stage, our most basic ideas about God are usually learned from our parents and/or society.

Stage 2: Mythic-Literal (mostly in school children): When children become school-age, they start understanding the world in more logical ways. They generally accept the stories told to them by their faith community but tend to understand them in very literal ways. [Some people remain in this stage through adulthood.]

Stage 3: Synthetic-Conventional (arising in adolescence; ages 12 to adulthood): Most people move on to this stage as teenagers. At this point, their lives have grown to include several different social circles, which they need to pull together. When this happens, a person usually adopts some sort of all-encompassing belief system. However, at this stage, people tend to have a hard time seeing outside their box, not recognizing that they are "inside" a belief system. At this stage, authority is usually placed in individuals or groups that represent one's beliefs. [A great many adults remain in this stage.]

Stage 4: Individuative-Reflective (usually mid-twenties to late thirties): This is the tough stage, often begun in young adulthood, when people start seeing outside the box and realizing that there are other "boxes." They begin to examine their beliefs critically on their own and often become disillusioned with their former faith. Ironically, the Stage 3 people usually think that Stage 4 people have become "backsliders" when in reality they have actually moved forward.

Stage 5: Conjunctive Faith (mid-life crisis): It is rare for people to reach this stage before mid-life. This is the point when people begin to realize the limits of logic and start to accept life's paradoxes. As they begin to see life as a mystery, they often return to sacred stories and symbols but this time without remaining in a theological box.

Stage 6: Universalizing Faith (enlightened stage): Few people reach this stage; those who do, live their lives to the full in service of others without real worry or spiritual doubt.

Models for Life's Journey

M. Scott Peck's Simplified Version (*A Different Drum*, 1987)

I. Chaotic-Antisocial – People in this stage are usually self-centered and often find themselves in trouble due to unprincipled living. If they do finally embrace the next stage, it often occurs in a very dramatic way.

II. Formal-Institutional – At this stage people rely on some sort of institution (such as a church) to give them stability. They become attached to the forms of their religion and become extremely upset when these are called into question.

III. Skeptic-Individual – Those who break with the previous stage usually do so when they start seriously questioning previously held values and beliefs. Frequently they end up non-religious and some stay here permanently.

IV. Mystical-Communal – People who reach this stage start to realize that there is truth to be found in the previous two stages and that life can be paradoxical and mysterious. Emphasis is placed more on community rather than on individual concerns.

5. James Hollis's Four Phases of Life

James Hollis, a Jungian analyst, notes that beyond the many subphases of life, there are four larges phases, each with a power to define the person's identity.[5] The first identity, *childhood*, is characterized by dependency of the ego on the actual world of the parents. The second identity begins at puberty. During *adolescence*, the emerging ego is malleable and prey to the influence of peers and pop culture. This phase has as its primary task the solidification of the ego, whereby the youth gains sufficient strength to leave parents, go into the larger world, and struggle for survival and the achievement of desire. Hollis calls the period from roughly twelve to forty the first adulthood. This identity, which may extend throughout one's life, is a provisional existence, lacking the depth and uniqueness that makes a person truly an individual.

At some point, when the projections and authority of the roles offered by society fail to meet the insurgence of the Self—that mysterious process within each of us that summons us to ourselves and which often manifests itself through symptoms such as loss of energy, depression, sudden fits of rage or over-consumption—one must confess to loss of control. The ego

---

5. This segment is adapted from Hollis, *Middle Passage*, 23–27.

never was in control but rather was driven by the energy of the parental and collective complexes sustained by the power of the projections onto the roles offered by society to those who would be adults. As long as the projections work, the individual manages to forestall the appointment with the inherent Self.[6]

The third phase of identity, the *second adulthood*, is launched when one's projections dissolve. In this crisis, this sense of betrayal, failed expectations, dissolution, and loss of meaning, one has the opportunity to become an individual, beyond the determinism of parents and cultural conditioning. Tragically, the repressive power of the psyche, with its reliance on authority, often keeps a person in thrall to cultural and parental complexes and thereby freezes development. Second adulthood is only attainable when the provisional identities have been discarded and the false self has died. The pain of such loss may be compensated by the rewards of the new life that follows, but the person in the midst of the midlife crisis may only experience the dying.

The fourth identity, *mortality*, involves learning to live with the mystery of death and accepting its reality.

Another way to look at these shifting identities is to classify their different axes. In the first identity, childhood, the operative axis is the parent-child relationship. In the first adulthood the axis lies between ego and world. The ego struggles to project itself into the world and create a world within the world. In the second adulthood, both during and after midlife, the axis connects ego and Self. It is natural for consciousness to assume that it knows all and is running the show. When its hegemony is overthrown, the humbled ego then begins the dialogue with the Self, defined as the mystery within, concerned with the purposiveness of the organism. The fourth axis is Self-God or Self-Cosmos. This axis is framed by the cosmic mystery that transcends the mystery of individual existence. Without some relationship to the cosmos, we are constrained to lives of transience, superficiality, and aridity. Since the dominant culture offers little mythic mediation for the placement of self in a larger context, it is all the more imperative that the individual enlarge his or her vision.

6. Bill Plotkin's Model of Human Development

In his book *Nature and the Human Soul* (2008), depth psychologist Bill Plotkin presents a nature-based model of human development called The

---

6. "Self" is capitalized to avoid confusing it with our ordinary, limited ego consciousness.

Wheel of Life, an eight-stage model that is both ecocentric and soulcentric, a nature-based model that fully honors the deeply imaginative potentials of the human psyche. A wilderness guide and self-styled "agent of cultural evolution," Plotkin uses his model to show how healthy and holistic lifestyles should be rooted in a childhood of innocence and wonder, sprout into an adolescence of creative fire and mystery-probing adventures, blossom into an authentic adulthood of cultural artistry and visionary leadership, and finally ripen into an elderhood of wisdom and grace, tending both the social and natural world. His premise is that true adulthood is rooted in mystical affiliation with nature, experienced as a sacred calling, embodied in soul-infused work and mature responsibilities. This mystical affiliation is the very core of maturity, and it is precisely what Plotkin believes has been overlooked or even suppressed by mainstream Western society.

The Wheel of Life model provides a means to support and quicken a foundational shift in worldview and values, from investment in the industrial growth society—which engenders an immature citizenry unable to imagine life beyond consumerism and soul-suppressing jobs—to intimacy with the natural world and with our souls. Building on new understandings from ecology, physics, ecopsychology, and related fields, Plotkin fosters a shift in human consciousness from egocentric (materialistic, anthropocentric, competition-based, class stratified, violence prone, and naturally unsustainable) to soulcentric (imaginative, ecocentric, cooperation based, just, compassionate, and sustainable) values, based on a deepening embrace of mystical traditions, both indigenous and Western.

Committed to promoting a global ecological citizenry, the Wheel of Life provides a model for the human life cycle based on eight acts, offering a map for reaching the destination of becoming fully human. The Wheel, ecocentric in that it models individual human development from the perspective of nature's cycles, rhythms, and patterns, is also soulcentric in that it envisions the principal goal of maturation to be the conscious discovery and embodiment of souls. Understanding the human soul as being the very core of human nature, the eight developmental stages—early childhood, middle childhood, early adolescence, late adolescence, early adulthood, late adulthood, early elderhood, late elderhood—together constitute a single story, the story of a deeply fulfilling but nevertheless entirely human life.

Part I – Developing a "Rule of Life"

Each stage features a nature-oriented and culture-oriented task, a gift, and a center of gravity, as seen in the following chart.

Stage	Title for Stage	Task	Gift	Center of Gravity
1. Early Childhood	The Innocent in the Nest	Ego formation and care of innocence	Luminous Presence	Spirit
2. Middle Childhood	The Explorer in the Garden	Discovering the natural world	Wonder	Family and nature
3. Early Adolescence	The Thespian at the Oasis	Creating a secure and authentic social self	Fire	Peer group, sex, and society
4. Late Adolescence	The Wanderer in the Cocoon	Leaving home (the adolescent identity) and exploring the mysteries	Mystery and darkness	The underworld
5. Early Adulthood	The Apprentice at the Wellspring	Learning delivery systems for embodying soul in culture	Visionary action and inspiration	Cultural depths

Models for Life's Journey

Stage	Title for Stage	Task	Gift	Center of Gravity
6. Late Adulthood	The Artisan in the Wild Orchard	Manifesting innovative delivery systems for soulwork	Seeds of cultural renaissance	Giveaway as art form
7. Early Elderhood	The Master in the Grove of Elders	Caring for the soul of the more-than-human community	Wholeness	Web of life
8. Late Elderhood	The Sage in the Mountain Cave	Tending the universe	Grace	Cosmos (spirit)

According to Plotkin, the eight stages, together with the passage from one stage to the next, are not defined by chronological age or social status but by the progress made with the developmental tasks encountered at each stage. Each transition involves loss and pain and entails a crisis for the conscious self. The stage of adolescence—beyond which most adults never move—holds the key to both individual development and human evolution. In this stage individuals develop their distinctive ego-based consciousness, which represents both their greatest liability as well as their greatest potential. If they are to become fully human and move to the stages of genuine adulthood, people in the adolescent stage must undergo an initiation process that requires letting go of the familiar and comfortable while submitting to a journey of descent into "the mysteries of nature and the human soul." Individuals who remain within the constraints of a largely adolescent world regress into "pathological adolescence," characterized by materialism, sexism, competitive violence, racism, egoism, and self-destructive patterns. Patho-adolescent societies are perpetuated by leaders and celebrities described as self-serving politicians, moralizing religious leaders, drug-induced entertainment icons, and greedy captains of industry. If society is going to develop soulcentrically, it must be overseen by councils of wise elders, not by assemblies of adolescent politicians and corporate officers.

To reiterate, Plotkin's stages, while correlating ideally with chronological, biological, and evolutionary age, are not primarily based on such phenomena, since people can remain locked in any of these stages, unable to progress further until they successfully complete the task(s) of that stage. According to Plotkin, one cannot skip a stage only to return later in hopes of moving on.

The story of the Wheel, like the phenomenon of second-half living, is significantly different from the one most contemporary people experience. In my estimation, Plotkin is mistaken in his insistence that humans cannot progress beyond their current stage until they successfully complete the tasks of that stage. This view is contrary to experience, overly deterministic, and ultimately unhelpful. The litmus test for progress into the second journey is not so much completing tasks as acquiring a nondualist state of awareness, which always includes and honors all previous stages. Once we have gained even momentary access to nondual unity, all previous stages can be revisited as needed, including our dualistic reason. In fact, our reason will have new freedom and clarity, because it is less needy; it does not need to be always right, self-sufficient, or convinced it embraces the whole picture. No matter how advanced or mystical our lives, there are always tasks, attitudes, and perceptions from the past that remain incomplete or inadequate during the second-half journey. Though they continue to define and shape us, they are transformable.

7. Richard Rohr's Levels of Spiritual Maturity

Citing Thomas Aquinas's observation that "Whatever is received is received according to the mode of the receiver," Rohr, a Franciscan priest and founder of the Center for Action and Contemplation in Albuquerque, New Mexico, notes that whatever one teaches or receives is heard on at least nine different levels, according to the inner, psychological, and spiritual maturity of the listener.[7] Level 1 people will misuse scripture, sacraments, and any other spiritual tool that is presented to them, whereas Level 7–9 people will "make lemonade out of even sour or unripe lemons." While discerning these levels from his own pastoral and teaching experience, Rohr is quick to note that his levels serve a didactic purpose; real life is much more subtle.

---

7. Rohr's list of nine levels, found below, is adapted from *Naked Now*, 164–66.

Models for Life's Journey

Rohr's list includes:

1. *My body and self-image are who I am.* Such a view represents dualistic/polarity thinking and leads to dominance of security, safety, and defensive needs.

2. *My external behavior is who I am.* People at this level need to look good to others, and in so doing hide or disguise contrary evidence from themselves and from others. This stage is common among conservatives.

3. *My thoughts/feelings are who I am.* People at this level develop intellect and will in order to have better thoughts and feelings, and in so doing control them to the extent that neither they nor others see their self-serving character. This education as a substitute for transformation is common among liberals and the educated.

4. *My deeper intuitions and felt knowledge are who I am.* This level, while a breakthrough from previous levels, keeps people stymied, for it substitutes individualism, self-absorption, and inner work for true encounter with otherness.

5. *My shadow self is who I am.* People at this level are overwhelmed by their own weakness; without guidance, grace, and prayer, many go back to previous identities.

6. *I am empty and powerless.* At this level most attempts to save the self by superior behavior, techniques, morality, positive roles, or religious devotion will lead to regression. All one can do is wait, ask, and trust. People at this level learn faith and discover the superior mentoring qualities of darkness. Such people are discovering for themselves the reality of God.

7. *I am much more than who I thought I was.* People at this level undergo the death of the false self and the birth of the True Self. Since such people are not yet at home here, their experience will feel like a void, even if a wonderful void. Such people, embarking on the second-half journey, are learning the meaning of "dark splendor."

8. *"I and the Father are one"* (John 10:30). At this level there is only God—or as Teresa of Avila states, "One knows God in oneself, and knows oneself in God." All else is seen as passing ego possession, which need not be protected, promoted, or proved—to anyone.

9. *I am who I am.* At this level one accepts oneself fully, warts and all; no window dressing is necessary. This level represents the most radical critique of religion, viewed now as just a pointer to reality and not reality itself. People at this stage need not appear to be anything but who they are. Fully detached from self-image, such people live in the image of God for themselves, which includes and loves both the good and the bad. Here one experiences total nonduality, the serenity and freedom of the saints.

For Rohr, the goal is to keep people moving deeper into faith, knowing they will receive all necessary information and experience at their level to travel onward.

CHAPTER 2

Types of Spirituality

Among all my patients in the second half of life—that is to say, over thirty-five—there has not been one whose problem in the last resort was not that of finding a religious outlook on life.

—CARL G. JUNG

LIKE CYCLISTS ON A tandem, personality and spirituality travel together through the journey of life. Riding in tandem, they are deeply influenced by conditions both internal (goals, moods, desires) and external to the self. When one leans, the other leans; where one starts, the other starts; if one stops, the other stops. Though not identical, they strive to be in sync, balancing one another in profound and intimate ways.[1] Personality takes the lead, and where personality goes, spirituality follows, though not blindly or passively. Spirituality has its own voice, and when its desires are addressed and heeded, personality thrives. When the two disagree, they must communicate, or the consequences can be disastrous. Cooperation always enhances the ride.

In this chapter you will have the opportunity to determine (or affirm) your personality type, as revealed by the Myers Briggs Type Indicator. In addition you will discover how your personality type influences your learning style, your spiritual journey, and your theological understanding. Like individuality, each person has a spirituality native to his or her own personality. Like personality, spirituality also yearns for growth and expression. While this guide makes no attempt to persuade you to join one or another organized religion or spiritual practice, it does provide, in this initial

---

1. This chapter is a revised and expanded version of Vande Kappelle's Appendix B, "Discovering Your Personality and Spirituality Type," *Iron Sharpens Iron*, 81–92.

session, valuable tools for discovering your psychological type and then for matching your personality characteristics with one of four spirituality types identified by religious scholars and found in various faith traditions.

Your spirituality, like your personality, can never be determined by someone else. It can be influenced by others, as in the case of parents and other authority figures. Ultimately, however, the choice of spirituality must be yours. And that's what the MBTI is about: choices.

Some history is in order. The famous Swiss psychologist Carl Gustav Jung published his work *Psychological Types* in 1923. Since he wrote in German for a largely specialized audience of psychologists, his theory of personality type found scant enthusiasm among ordinary people interested in personality theory. Two women, Isabel Myers and her mother Katherine Cook Briggs, followed Jung's theory with interest for about sixteen years when the Second World War broke out. The war effort took many men from the industrial workforce and brought many women out of their normal activities to replace them. The two women sought for a type indicator that might identify the kind of job for the war effort that non specialists could perform naturally and effectively. The result became the MBTI, a questionnaire that sorted people into one of sixteen possible personality types in terms of Jungian type theory. In 1923, when Myers and Briggs produced the first set of questions destined to become the MBTI, the academic community questioned its validity, in part because it had little familiarity and therefore little use for Jung's theory of psychological type. Undaunted, Isabel Myers devoted the entire second half of her life to interpreting and adapting Jung's theory, helping normal people understand their uniqueness, particularly in terms of the way they take in and process information.

Now, over a half century later, many Jungian concepts are widely known and accepted and millions have taken the MBTI, which is widely applied in team building, organization development, business management, education, and career counseling. Understanding one's type is making a welcome change in people's lives globally, in a wide diversity of situations.

Discovering Your Personality Type

If you have never taken the MBTI, or if you need to verify your personality type, I recommend that you take the online version of the test.[2] But

---

2. To find your type, go to www.humanmetrics.com and click on "Jung Typology Test" and then "Take Test." Either before or after taking the test, click on the Full

Types of Spirituality

before you do, keep in mind that the MBTI is not really a test but a sorter of preferences in four categories. There is no "right" or "wrong" answer. In order to get accurate results, adopt a relaxed demeanor and remember that you are attempting to discover your preferred answer to each question, not what you or your parents or anyone else wished you preferred as an answer. Since humans are complex individuals, our preferences may vary from situation to situation. The MBTI reports preferences on four scales, each consisting of two opposite poles. The following exercise conveys what Jung and Myers meant by "preferences":

First, on the line below sign your name as you normally do;

_____

Now, sign your name again on the line below, but this time use your other hand;

_____

The first result was effortless and natural, the second awkward and unnatural. Similarly, according to the theory, everyone has a natural preference for one of the two opposites on each of the four MBTI scales. You use both preferences at different times, but not both at once and not, in most cases, with equal confidence.

At the conclusion of the test you will receive four letters, which comprise your personality type. They indicate the differences in people that result from

- where they prefer to focus their attention (Extraversion or Introversion) – E or I;
- the way they prefer to take in information (Sensing or Intuition) – S or N;
- the way they prefer to make decisions (Thinking or Feeling) – T or F;
- how they orient themselves to the external world (Judging or Perceiving) – J or P.

These preferences produce sixteen different kinds of people, interested in different things and drawn to different fields. Each type has its own inherent strengths as well as its likely blind spots. As I mentioned earlier, discovering

---

Description link for clarification of the Jungian terminology and concepts. Once you have completed the 72 questions, click "Score It" at the bottom to obtain your results. The entire exercise will take 10 to 15 minutes. For further analysis and potential verification of your personality type, consult www.personalitypathways.com/type-inventory.html.

one's personality type is extremely beneficial, for it influences career choices, marriage choices, learning style, spiritual journeys, theological understanding, and so much more.

For the moment, let's examine learning styles associated with each preference, since inclinations at this dimension impact choices at other cognitive, relational, and intuitive levels.

Extraverts

Learn best when in action

Value physical activity

Like to study with others

Prefer discussion

Introverts

Learn best by pausing to think

Value reading

Prefer to study individually

Prefer clear lectures

Sensors

Seek specific information

Observe specific facts

Follow practical interests

Prefer step-by-step instructions

Like hands-on experience

Trust material as presented

Seek mentors who give clear teaching

Intuitives

Seek quick insights

Use imagination to go beyond facts

Follow intellectual interests

Create their own directions

Like theories to give perspective

Read between the lines

Seek mentors who encourage independent thinking

Thinkers

Want objective material to study

Logic guides learning

Like to critique new ideas

Can easily find flaws in an argument

Feelers

Want to relate to the material personally

Personal values important

Like to please instructors

Can easily find something to appreciate

Learn by challenge and debate

Learn by being supported and appreciated

Want mentors who make logical presentations

Want mentors who establish personal rapport

Judgers	**Perceivers**
Like formal instructions for solving problems	Like to solve problems informally
Value dependability	Value change
Plan work well in advance	Work spontaneously
Work steadily toward goals	Work impulsively with bursts of energy
Prefer prescribed tasks	Prefer adaptive tasks
Drive toward closure	Stay open to new information
Want instructors to be organized	Want instructors to be inspiring

Using combinations of preferences also yields interesting results on the topic of learning styles. Combining the first two letters of your type reveals some interesting patters. The first two letters show where you prefer to focus your attention and how you prefer to take in information. For example, ES types are usually more interested in the practical usefulness of learning, while IN types are usually more interested in abstractions and learning for its own sake. College samples of type distributions reveal widespread discrepancies between faculty and students in terms of teaching and learning preference. Whereas a majority of college faculty fall into the IN and EN categories, ES and IS types predominate among college students.

Using the second and last letters of one's type is also a useful way to think about learning style. The second letter (S or N) describes whether one prefers to focus on facts and reality (Sensing) or abstract concepts and theories (Intuition). The last letter (J or P) indicates whether one prefers to decide on that information quickly and then move on (Judging) or keep open to new information (Perceiving). College samples indicate that there are three times as many students who prefer Sensing and Perceiving as there are faculty with this combination. SP students prefer a flexible approach to factual material. Their NJ professors, on the other hand, prefer structure and theories. The SP students are more likely to view the facts themselves as more important than the theories and are less likely to want the facts organized according to some grand structure. No matter which preference combination one examines, however, it is clear that Sensing types will probably need to learn to cope with the Intuitive environment preferred by the majority of their professors.

This information, when applied to educational and liturgical settings, might presumably uncover a similar disconnect between academically trained clergy and laypersons on at least two fronts: (a) in terms of teaching and learning preference as well as (b) in terms of theological appreciation and understanding.

Type Dynamics and Development

Looking at the world from the standpoint of type provides a framework for deeper understanding of oneself and others. The next level of exploration consists of two general areas of type theory: (1) type dynamics, which examines the interaction among the preferences, and (2) type development, which suggests the probable path of development and growth for each type.

Type Dynamics: Determining Dominance

Of the two middle letters in your type (S or N, T or F), one will be your dominant function, your home base of operations; the other will be your auxiliary, your second most important function. The following formula determines how to locate these functions; it is a bit tricky at first, so study it carefully until you understand it:

> To locate your dominant, look to the fourth letter of your personality type (J or P). This will tell you how you extravert, whether with your perceiving function (S or N) or with your judging function (T or F). Then look at the first letter (E or I) of your personality type. If you prefer Extraversion, how you extravert will be your dominant function. If you prefer Introversion, then the other letter will be your dominant.

For example, for ESTJ, the last letter (J) points to the judging function, which is T; since this person is an Extravert, T is the dominant function, with S as the auxiliary. In an opposite example, INFP, the last letter

(P) points to the perceiving function, which is N; that is how this person extraverts. However, since this person prefers Introversion, the F is the introverted dominant function and N is the auxiliary.

Our dominant function is important to our spirituality because it will lead us as we prepare for the journey, as we navigate the journey, and as we reengage with the elements of our faith along the way. But it will be refined and balanced for a greater wholeness in collaboration with the auxiliary. In order to include all four mental functions (S, N, T, and F), Jung established a hierarchy that he labeled the dominant, auxiliary, tertiary, and inferior functions. The tertiary function is usually much less developed and conscious than the first two. It is the opposite of the auxiliary. The inferior function, the opposite of the dominant function, has received the least energy and attention and therefore is the least developed. According to Jungian theory, the inferior function is the primary connection to the unconscious and the most difficult to use in one's conscious life. Under stress or crisis, when our dominant is not coping well in our conscious life, often the inferior will kick in, bringing with it lots of chaotic perceptions or judgments. At this point people will see us at our worst.

Our less-preferred functions, especially the inferior, are vital to integrate the self because they access the rich depth available in the unconscious. The inferior function is therefore our greatest source for learning about new sides of ourselves and alternative potentialities to complement those strengths we currently possess. Avenues for spiritual growth are discovered in those moments when we are off balance and vulnerable. In these moments great insights for personal and spiritual growth arise.

Type Development

When people are young, their energy is directed toward development of their most preferred, dominant function, and their behavior reflects this. An introverted Feeling child will be a quiet observer, with an instinctive sense of others' feelings; an introverted Intuitive child will be actively exploring the variety of the surrounding world. An extraverted Thinking child will try to order his environment to fit with his logical principles; an introverted Thinking child will try to internally make sense of her world. Once children develop skills in their dominant function, the focus of energy and attention then shifts to the auxiliary function. The primary task of type development in the first part of life is to establish the leadership provided by the dominant function, balanced by the healthy development of the auxiliary function. Later in life, the focus of development shifts again, this time to the less-preferred functions, aspects of the individual's personality and potential that have only minimally been explored. This redirection of energy is part of the midlife transition, which Jung saw as the gateway to later life development and satisfaction. The task of the second half of life, then, is to move toward full development of all of oneself, including those parts that were previously neglected and unrealized.

When people first learn Jung's theory, they often think the ideal is to develop all four functions with equal facility to achieve balance. That, however, is not how development works, for if a person tries to develop opposite ways of perceiving equally, for example, then neither Sensing nor Intuition will receive the focus or attention necessary to become fully reliable. The four functions tend to pull in opposite directions: Sensing, to the reality of the present; Intuition, to the possibility of the future; Thinking, to decisions based on objective logic; and Feeling, to decisions based on subjective values. People who do not establish dominance of each pair of functions are inconsistent in their behavior, pulled first in one direction and then another. The goal of type development, then, is not equal development and use of all the functions, but rather the ability to use each mental process with some facility when it is appropriate.

In conclusion, Jung's model of the human journey is based on the following assumptions:

- each person has an innate urge to grow;
- the human psyche is self-regulating and capable of healing itself;
- development means developing conscious control over and facility in the use of a function;
- development is an interaction between a person's innate type preferences and the environment. If the environment is supportive, growth tends to follow innate type. If the environment is not supportive, the pattern may be affected by a person's adaptation to the requirements of the environment;
- in the first half of life, growth takes the form of development of the preferred functions; in the second half of life, a person's focus of energy and attention naturally shifts to the less-preferred functions. This is a process of moving toward one's unexplored potential.

Types of Spirituality

The following quote summarizes Jung's understanding of the psychological-spiritual task during the second half of life: "Among all my patients in the second half of life—that is to say, over thirty-five—there has not been one whose problem in the last resort was not that of finding a religious outlook on life." We are beginning to comprehend his meaning.

Typology and Spirituality

Each person is unique, with a distinct personality. Despite their uniqueness, individuals share personality traits, qualities, and preferences that can be defined and typed into distinct categories. That, as we have seen, is the premise upon which the MBTI is built. These insights have a remarkable correlation with spirituality, as we discover in the following inter-related typologies.

1. Hindu Typology

Huston Smith, widely regarded as the foremost authority on the history of religions, noted in his classic text, *The World's Religions*,[3] that ancient Hindu scholars identified four basic spiritual personality types: some people are primarily reflective, some are basically emotional, others are essentially active, and yet others are experimentally inclined. While the types should not be regarded inflexibly, since human beings possess all four abilities to some degree, each person prefers one style over the rest. Carl Jung seems to have built his typology of personality on this Indian model, with some modifications. For each of these personality types Hinduism prescribes a distinct yoga or spiritual path that capitalizes on the type's distinctive strength:

- Karma yoga, intended for persons of active bent, is *the path through work*. The best way for persons on this path to express their spirituality is to perform action selflessly, for the sake of God and others instead of their own. In this way tasks become sacralized; work becomes worship. The aim is to channel the love that lies at the base of one's heart through disinterested action, detached from any consequences benefitting self-interest;

- Bhakti yoga, requiring a rare combination of rationality and spirituality, is *the path of devotion*. It is intended for those whose lives are

---

3. This volume was first published in 1958 as *The Religions of Man* and then revised in 1991 under its current title.

powered primarily by emotion, the strongest of which is love. The aim is to channel the love that lies at the base of one's heart through relationship;

- Jnana yoga, intended for those who possess a strong reflective bent, is *the path of knowledge*. While thinking is important for such people, it has less to do with factual information than with insight or discernment regarding knowledge. The aim is to channel the love that lies at the base of one's heart through understanding;

- Raja yoga, intended for those who are scientifically or experimentally inclined, is *the path of liberation* (mystical union). Raja seeks freedom through self-actualization. The aim is to channel the love that lies at the base of one's heart through psychophysical (mental) experiments that culminate in harmony, freedom, and integration, leading the practitioner to direct personal experience of "the beyond that is within."

2. Richardson's Typology

Building on the insights of psychological type theory developed by Carl Jung and Isabel Briggs Myer, globetrotting minister and author Peter Tufts Richardson notes that four different approaches to human spirituality emerge from the MBTI.[4] How we perceive the world and how we respond to it (how we judge) seems to be directly connected to the spiritual path we find most personally satisfying. Utilizing the principle that one's spirituality flows out of one's individuality, Richardson locates the key to spirituality in the two middle letters of one's personality type. These cognitive pairs result in four possibilities: ST, SF, NT, and NF. One of these pairs defines each person's spirituality.

Richardson defines the four spirituality types, describes qualities and patterns unique to each path, and identifies mentors from different world religions for each journey:

ST – Journey of Works (Moses)

SF – Journey of Devotion (Muhammad)

NT – Journey of Unity (Buddha)

NF – Journey of Harmony (Jesus)

---

4. His approach is described in *Four Spiritualities*.

Types of Spirituality

STs are characterized by a *task-oriented spirituality*. ST youth are drawn to activities that are task-oriented, such as team sports. And often they will be leaders. They may help with chores around the house, but they are not particularly swayed by the desires of a parent. They learn by experience, wanting to discover things for themselves; they need to know why things are required and how they work. As teens STs divide into two groups: the freedom lovers (STPs) and the responsible ones (STJs), but all are oriented around well-defined institutions. When they grow up, STs become the realists, always in touch with the facts, unbiased, objective, accurate, paying attention to relevant details. They are skilled administrators, responsible, consistent, efficient, and analytical. The Journey of Works is practical and involves a lifetime of effort; people on this path like to follow procedures efficiently, often legalistically. Work is the means for meeting all obligations and responsibilities. It gives life dignity and results in solid citizenship. STs commit themselves to the building up and maintaining of institutions, reliably and loyally. They prefer direct, experience-based, often physical activities, working with their hands or otherwise directly in situations, trying out procedures to see what works best, often preferring technical tasks to those requiring people skills. They learn best on the job, noticing relevant details, collecting facts, and verifying them directly by the senses. They arrive at conclusions in a linear cause-and-effect way. Their opinions, based on their experience, will often be firmly held and based on common sense. A confusion of beliefs is intolerable for STs. They like to find a world in balance, with reliable structures that lead them toward the right way to go. For the Journey of Works, order and a clear message are essential conditions. Appreciating clear beliefs and reliable structure, they tend to be literalists and legalists in religion; commitment provides religion stability.

ST mentors include Confucius, Clement of Alexandria, Origen of Alexandria, Augustine, Ignatius of Loyola, Martin Luther, Brother Lawrence, George Washington, and Gandhi; biblical mentors include Ruth, Abigail, Martha of Bethany, and Peter.

SFs are characterized by an *experience-based spirituality*. SF youth make friends easily, avoid conflict, and desire to please. They thrive in well-structured environments and when expectations are clear. They need to be reassured when they are on the right track and rewarded for good behavior. As adults SFs are sensitive, loyal, and caring; they live responsibly as parents and citizens and are devoted to serving others in tangible ways. In the

Part I – Developing a "Rule of Life"

Journey of Devotion, living in the immediate present is central. Instead of the cosmic, the tangible task at hand is the focus. Details are important. Stressing continuity and propriety, SFs are traditionalists. In their communications they prefer anecdotes, stories, and tangible references to symbolic or abstract reasoning. Practical and interactive, they take a tactile, hands-on approach to the spiritual life.

SF mentors include St. Benedict, St. Francis, Julian of Norwich, John Wesley, and Ramakrishna; biblical mentors include Esther, Mary Magdalene, Nicodemus, Mary of Bethany, and the disciple John, son of Zebedee.

NTs are characterized by a *highly principled spirituality*. NT youth value their independence and tend to work hard to establish their competence in the challenges they decide to tackle. Uncomfortable with abstraction, they often ask why, and if the answers they receive are unsatisfactory, they may set out to improve upon them or else to rebel against arbitrary answers. As adults NTs tend to enjoy solving problems, love to exchange ideas, or stimulate new efforts. Searching for unifying solutions, they appreciate speculative theories that lead to intellectual clarity. In the Journey of Unity, the search for truth or the quest for perfection is often as satisfying as the conclusions reached along the way. NTs are foremost change agents and strategic planners. On account of their critical nature, they may be perceived by others, particularly SFs, as stubborn or uncooperative. Along with principles and truth, individuals on this path are also distinguished by vision and concern for social justice.

NT mentors include Socrates, St. Dominic, Thomas Aquinas, John Calvin, Albert Schweitzer, Dorothy Day, Martin Luther King Jr., Elie Weisel, Albert Einstein, and Ralph Nader; biblical mentors include Amos, Deborah, and Paul.

NFs are characterized by a *questing spirituality*. NF youth like to please the adults and peers in their live. They can be easily crushed by disapproval or even indifference. They need regular affirmation from parents and teachers if their self-esteem and self-image are not to suffer. Because they see possibilities in the future (N) and like to gain approval from others, they often will prepare for careers and causes in response to adult mentors in their lives. NF youth are exceedingly idealistic. Their idealism is often unpredictable; some young men may overcompensate for their F by expressing their idealism in hostile ways. They are strongly represented among protestors for social issues. NF adults are enthusiastic and insightful, recognizing the personal needs of others. Idealists by nature, they always see a way to make life better. They have an ability to draw people into a discussion and to facilitate consensus-building for social harmony and good. NFs on a healthy track will regularly draw others toward their own best selves. The Intuitive proclivity for symbol and metaphor, combining with global vision for the wellbeing of the world, makes NFs inspired communicators of the ideal. Future-oriented and attuned to the big picture of life as a whole, people on the Journey of Harmony tend to focus more on possibilities than on concrete situations at hand. Their N nature is balanced, however, by their F side, which keeps them in touch with reality and keeps their utopian bent in check. Flexible and open to change, NFs see life as continual self-creating process, a quest toward selfhood. Their malleable natures exist to be formed and re-formed in ever more exquisite patterns of self-actualization. NFs seek increasing meaning and spiritual purpose in life.

NF mentors include Meister Eckhart, Teresa of Avila (also SF and ST), St. John of the Cross, Thoreau, Walt Whitman, Tagore, Thomas Merton, George Fox (Quakers); biblical mentors include Abraham, Joseph, Miriam, and Mary (mother of Jesus).

3. Holmes's Typology

Urban Holmes, dean of the School of Theology at The University of the South in Sewanee, Tennessee from 1973 until his death in 1981, presents a helpful typology for the spiritual life in his insightful book *A History of Spirituality*. His book provides a tool and a method by which to conceptualize and name spiritual experience within a basic framework, particularly useful in helping to position one's own religious experience within the context of the experience of others.

Holmes suggests two appropriate ends for the spiritual life: a speculative spirituality that focuses on the illumination of the mind and an affective spirituality that focuses on the illumination of the heart. He further suggests two appropriate means toward those ends: a kataphatic means—an indirect way of knowing in which our relationship with God is mediated—and an apophatic means—a direct way of knowing, in which our relationship with God is not mediated.

Holmes calls his model the "Circle of Sensibility," and in it he delineates four styles of prayer, later configured as schools of spirituality. By "sensibility" he refers to the possibilities within individuals and communities as they seek to understand the experience of God and its meaning for our times. Holmes proposes the use of two intersecting lines placed within

Part I – Developing a "Rule of Life"

a circle. The vertical line creates a north-south axis, with Sensibility (Mind or Intellect) at the north pole and Affective (Heart or Emotion) at the south pole. The horizontal line creates an east-west axis, with Kataphatic (God as Revealed: known through images) at the east pole and Apophatic (God as Mystery: known mystically). Below is an adaptation of his circle, divided into four quadrants. Each quadrant contains one of the four schools of spirituality, which he labeled "speculative-kataphatic" (Type I spirituality), affective-kataphatic (Type II spirituality), affective-apophatic (Type III spirituality), and speculative-apophatic (Type IV spirituality).

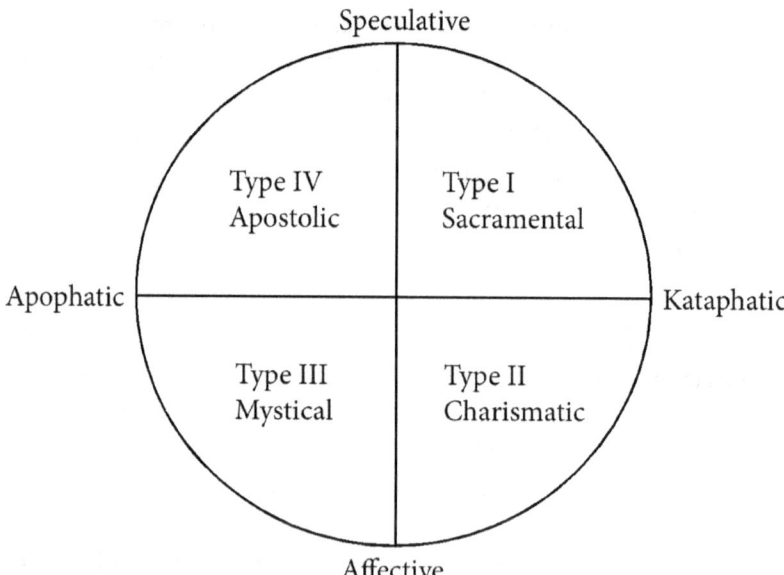

Type I spirituality, an intellectual "thinking" spirituality, has been identified as "sacramental." Its primary aim is to aid persons in fulfilling their vocation in the world. This spirituality favors what it can see, touch, and vividly imagine. Type II spirituality, a sensate, heartfelt approach to spirituality, has been identified as "charismatic." Its primary aim is to achieve holiness of life through personal renewal. Type III spirituality, which emphasizes being and direct experience of God, has been identified as "mystical." Its primary aim is union with the Holy, an unattainable goal, a journey that nevertheless continually impels the disciple onward. Type IV spirituality, a visionary, almost crusading type of spirituality, has been identified as "apostolic." Its primary aim is to obey God's will completely. Its major concerns are witness to God's reign and striving for justice and peace.

It is clear that Holmes's typology overlaps significantly with Jung's typology, as incorporated in the MBTI, and that it is compatible with Richardson's adaptation and analysis of the four spirituality types. In his description of the four "schools" of spirituality, Holmes cautions against excess, for each of these approaches appears subject to a distortion or natural "heresy." A heresy is a truth that goes too far, denying its countertruth.

Type I spirituality (the speculative-kataphatic approach) falls prey to the "heresy" of rationalism (*an excessive concern for right thinking* that leads to dogmatism) if it denies the validity or counterbalance of Type III spirituality (affective-apophatic), its diagonal (opposite) approach. Each approach should look to its diagonal spirituality for growth and balance. Type II spirituality (the affective-kataphatic approach) risks falling into the "heresy" of pietism, *an excessive concern for right feelings* that leads to emotionalism. Type III spirituality (the affective-apophatic approach) is subject to the "heresy" of quietism, *an excessive concern for right internal experience* that leads to escapism or withdrawal; and Type IV spirituality (the speculative-apophatic approach) may fall into the "heresy" of encratism, *an excessive concern for right behavior* that leads to moralism. Each approach, then, needs to be held in tension with its opposite.

The understanding of spirituality provided by these typologies results in great benefit to one's spiritual identity as well to the level and nature of engagement with one's worshipping community. For example, from this fountain flow insights concerning one's approach to worship, prayer, and meditation.

Type I spirituality produces theological reflection and crafts position papers. Its practitioners are analytical, apprehending theology as doctrine. Divine guidance comes chiefly through scripture and sermons. Worship is orderly and patterned. Reading is central to this spirituality. Prayer in this quadrant is word-based and thought-out, whether aloud or silent. Theological discussion is common with this type, but if not balanced with other activities, can lead to a one-dimensional "head trips."

Type II spirituality uses an entirely different spiritual "vocabulary" in expressing its heartfelt intuition. Since experience must be shared, its adherents often emphasize evangelism, and personal transformation, sometimes of a sudden type. Witnessing, testimonials, and especially music mark congregational worship. Theologically this approach stresses immanence over the transcendence of God. Friendship with Jesus and an outpouring of the Spirit provide signs of God's presence in life. Type II prayer is often word-based but stated extemporaneously. Worship is full of feeling, energy, and bodily freedom of expression that Type I worship generally lacks. African-American churches have this capacity for spontaneity and enthusiastic worship. Not only in the U.S. but also worldwide, many Christians formerly concentrated in Type I mainline denominations are now leaving and, where they seek corporate worship, are moving to congregations that represent more affective (charismatic) types of worship.

Type III spirituality is dominated by contemplative prayer, the purpose of which is not to fill the mind or express the mind as to free the mind. The goal is to empty the self from all distractions so as to be fully receptive. Classic Christian congregational approaches may be found in Quaker worship, which silences the senses to create empty space, and Eastern Orthodox worship, which makes use of the senses as a means of eliminating their influence. While Orthodox utilize icons, music, and incense as vehicles for the mystery spiritually present but hidden, Quakers eliminate sermons, clergy, and sacraments altogether, emphasizing hearing rather than speaking. This form of worship attracts people who are by nature contemplative, introspective, intuitive, and inner directed. Representatives of this approach, often uncomfortable with organized religion, find simple life styles appealing. Historically, Type III spirituality has pushed the frontiers of theology in the West, providing rich fodder for predominantly Type I spirituality.

Type IV spirituality, which combines mystic experience with an intellectual mode of gathering data, attracts single-minded visionaries with a deeply focused spirituality. Practitioners of this mode of spirituality care less than do others about affiliation with organized religion, certainly less than those in types I and II. Their aim is to obey God. Theirs is a courageous idealism that takes responsibility for change, creating a passion for transforming society. Type IV practitioners equate prayer and theology with action. What other spirituality schools might consider a response to prayer (obedience), this school considers as actual prayer. Disciples on this path often participate in marches and rallies and seek to serve in the Peace Corps or locally in organizations such as AmeriCorps. Taking as their motto the words of Jesus in Matthew 25:40: "Truly I tell you, just as you do it to one of the least of these . . . you do it to me," they associate worship and prayer with the presence of God, particularly evident in situations of human need.

Types of Spirituality

As we sort for personality and spirituality types, we need to keep in mind that no two people are identical, even when they share the same characteristics. Some show a clear preference for a particular function, others a moderate or even a weak preference. Persons who share the same characteristics may, in fact, be quite different. Individuals who sort into the same spirituality type, based on their perceiving or judging functions, are further distinguished by their other cognitive functions: their life attitudes (E or I) and their life orientations (J or P). Further, all of us can learn to use the opposite functions. These psychological types, like the schools of spirituality, are not boxes into which we can place people. They are simply typologies that can help us better understand ourselves and others, especially those who are different from us.

Many texts attempt to find correlation between the Myers-Briggs categories and the four schools of spirituality. If one assumes that the four poles correlate with the four middle functions—the speculative pole with T, affective with F, kataphatic with S, and apophatic with N—the results place STs in the speculative-kataphatic (Type I) quadrant, the SFs in the affective-kataphatic (Type II), the NFs in the affective-apophatic (Type III), and the NTs in the speculative-apophatic (Type IV). While attractive for its simplicity, this solution has its detractors, including John Westerhoff, long-time professor at Duke University Divinity School, who supports Jung's contention that only the stronger of the two middle traits (our dominant function) is a useful indicator of behavior (see the discussion above on "type dynamics"). According to this insight, four categories are available: T, S, N, and F. From this perspective, the schools of spirituality and personality types configure like this:

- the speculative-kataphatic (Type I) quadrant = S
- the affective-kataphatic (Type II) quadrant = F
- the affective-apophatic (Type III) quadrant = N
- the speculative-apophatic (Type IV) quadrant = T

Jung offers another insight. He suggests that in our lives we need to differentiate between work and leisure; if our personality needs are met in our work, we will seek their opposite in our leisure. This is another way of affirming that in our lives—physically, emotionally, and spiritually—as we move back and forth from dominant quadrants to diagonal quadrants, we will discover beneficial pathways for personal growth.

Part I – Developing a "Rule of Life"

Temperament and Personality

People are naturally different from one another in fundamental ways: they want different things, have different aims, think and learn differently, and believe differently. And of course, how they act and emote is governed by individual needs, desires, and beliefs. In many cases, differences in others trigger a negative response. Seeing others differing from us, we conclude that when they differ in behavior or response, it is due to some malady or flaw. Our job, at least for those near us, would seem to be to correct their flaws, making those near us more like us. Such a task, however, is doomed from the start. Our attempts to change others, whether spouse, sibling, lover, co-worker or friend, can culminate in change, but the result is a distortion and not a transformation. Besides, trying to change them is futile and counterproductive, in that most of the differences are essentially good.

The belief that people are fundamentally alike appears to be a twentieth century notion. The idea is probably related to the growth of democracy in the Western world. If we are equals, we must be alike. Classical psychologists such as Freud, Adler, Sullivan, Fromm and their followers affirmed the idea of singular motivation. Whatever the drive, whether motivated by Eros, power, social solidarity, or the search after Self, each personality school made one instinct primary for everybody.

Carl Jung disagreed. He noted that people differ in fundamental ways, even though they all possess the same instincts to drive them from within. No instinct is more important; what is important is our preference for how we function. Our preference for a given function is characteristic, and so we may be "typed" by this preference.

The developments of psychology in the twentieth century were amazing. Behaviorists, cognitivists, constructivists and others studied the nature of human beings. Most of these theories tried to answer the question whether human personality is determined by nature (i.e. heredity) or nurture (i.e. environment or learning). Theories that claimed human personality is a function of nature (or heredity) are called temperament theories. Temperament is that aspect of our personalities that is genetically based and therefore innate. That does not mean that a temperament theory rules out the role of environment; rather, a temperament theory does not focus on environment. It should also be noted that the issue of temperament is much older than psychology itself. It has a history of at least five thousand years.

People's involvement with the notion of "temperament" can be traced back to the traditions of ancient Egypt and Mesopotamia, where the health of the human body was considered to be connected with the four basic elements of nature—air, soil, water, and fire. The four elements, in turn, were related to body fluids (also called humors). In ancient Greek medicine, Hippocrates (c. 370 BC) was the first to classify people according to their dominant body fluids: blood, black bile, phlegm, and yellow bile. The density of the fluids within individuals was believed to determine their personality. For Hippocrates, people could be classified as "cheerful," "somber," "calm," or "enthusiastic." The Roman physician Galen (c. AD 190), who developed the ideas of Hippocrates, constructed a taxonomy of human behavior combining the four basic elements of nature with a matrix of hot/cold and dry/wet. Where all the elements were balanced, the individual was said to possess a balanced personality. Another possibility was that one element dominated the rest. This resulted in four less-balanced personality types, which Galen called Sanguine, Melancholic, Phlegmatic, and Choleric.

The sanguine individual, in which blood predominates, is claimed to be cheerful and optimistic, pleasant to be with, and comfortable with his or her work. The melancholic type, in which black bile or gall predominates, is said to be sad, depressed, and pessimistic. The phlegmatic type, in which phlegm predominates, is said to be slow, dull, and calm. The choleric type, said to have an excess of bile, is quick, passionate, hot-tempered, and often aggressive. While we might question the specifics of Galen's bodily fluids, the personal element seems to have some merit, for we all know individuals that fit one of these four temperaments, particularly if we replace Galen's terms with more familiar ones: sanguine with cheerful, melancholic with broody, phlegmatic with calm, and choleric with excitable.

Nearly six hundred years before Galen, Plato had written in *The Republic* of four kinds of character that clearly corresponded with the four temperaments attributed to Hippocrates. Plato was more interested in the individual's contribution to the social than in underlying temperament, and so he named the Sanguine temperament the Artisan, endowed with artistic sense (driven by imagery and likely drawn to the arts, crafts, and creativity in general) and playing an aesthetic role in society. He named the Melancholic temperament the Guardian, endowed with common sense (driven by honor, duty, and trust in others and drawn to traditional leadership roles) and playing a caretaking role in society. He named the Phlegmatic temperament the Rationalist, endowed with reasoning ability (driven by cold and calm reason and likely drawn to logical, mathematical fields) and playing the role of logical investigator in society. And he named the Choleric temperament the Idealist, endowed with intuitive sensibility (driven by intuition and insight and likely drawn to activities involving ethics, relationships, and establishing harmony) and playing a moral role in society. A generation after Plato, Aristotle defined character in terms of happiness and not, as his mentor Plato had done, in terms of virtue. Aristotle identified four sources of happiness: sensual pleasure, acquiring assets, logical investigation, and moral virtue.

Writing about the year 180 AD, Irenaeus, Bishop of Lyons correlated the four gospels with the four living creatures of Ezekiel 1 and Revelation 4 as well as to four chief characteristics of Christ himself. The gospel according to Matthew corresponds to the Man, because it emphasizes Christ's humanity, especially by beginning with his genealogy; Mark corresponds to the Lion, because it emphasizes Christ's divine kingship; Luke corresponds to the Bull, because in this gospel Christ is presented as the servant and the sacrificial offering on behalf of sin; and John corresponds to the Eagle, because its clarity of vision pierces the highest things. Though not explicit in Irenaeus, these groups of four can be correlated to the four temperaments quite easily. While Irenaeus doesn't specifically draw the connection between Plato's temperaments and the Four Evangelists (gospels), he does adopt Plato's system, giving the four temperaments his own labels, which are more behaviorally and less role-oriented. Artisans he labeled "spontaneous," Guardians he called "historical," Rationals he termed "scholarly," and Idealists he named "spiritual."

These ancient claims survived until the twentieth century, when they found their way to modern psychology. Modern psychologists proposed their own views of the four temperaments and coined different terms to refer to them. Although the terms used by each psychologist may differ from the ones used by others, they present essentially the same ideas. In 1905 Erich Adickes said that humans are divided into four world views: Innovative, Traditional, Skeptical, and Doctrinaire. In 1914 Eduard Spränger wrote of four "value attitudes" that distinguish one personality from another: Artistic, Economic, Theoretic, and Religious. A few years later Ernst Kretschmer took a slightly different approach and proposed that both normal and abnormal behavior can be understood in terms of four "character styles": Hypomanic, Depressive, Anesthetic, and Hyperesthetic. In 1947 Eric Fromm attributed four different "orientations" to the four styles: Exploitative, Hoarding, Marketing and Receptive. That same year Hans Eysenck, best known for his work on intelligence and personality, identified two major dimensions of human personality: Neuroticism (the tendency to experience negative emotions) and Extraversion (the tendency to enjoy positive events, especially social ones). Upon pairing these two dimensions, he noted that the results were similar to the four ancient temperaments.

Not surprisingly, the categories we have thus far established (humors, temperaments, drives, societal roles, sources of happiness, living creatures, gospels, value attitudes, character styles, orientations) were eventually seen as corresponding to other groups of four like the seasons, the major organs, the four elements, and the four Hindu yogas.

Keirsey Typology

Beginning with the publication of his book *Please Understand Me* (co-authored with Marilyn Bates in 1978), clinical psychologist David Keirsey combined the personality theory of Isabel Myers and Katherine Briggs (MBTI) with the insights of the temperament hypothesis. While building on the MBTI behavioral descriptions, he subordinated Jung's idea of "function" or "type" to the concept of "temperament," noting that the latter has a much wider range as an explainer of behavior. While knowing a person's type has great value for anticipating behavior, the concept of temperament is said to be broader in scope, denoting a unification of otherwise disparate forces. Unlike Jungian typology, in which types are built through combination of "functions," temperament theory views types as emerging from temperaments by way of differentiation. A person becomes an ENFJ or INFP, for example, because of a given temperament rather than because extraversion or introversion somehow combined with intuition. Thus temperament theory replaces the principles of integration (viewed as reductionist) with the principle of differentiation. According to this theory, temperament determines behavior because behavior is the instrument for getting what one must have, satisfying the desire for that primary necessity that drives our personality, whether it be the hunger for power, status, freedom, or meaning.

Utilizing MBTI functions, Kiersey names his four temperaments after four Greek gods, all of whom Zeus commissioned to make humans more like the gods:, Dionysus, to teach humans joy, Epimetheus, to convey a sense of duty, Prometheus, to give humans science, and Apollo, to give humans a sense of spirit. The four temperaments are labeled as follows:

1. *Dionysian* or *SPs* (a combination of Sensing and Perceiving, namely ISTP, ESTP, ISFP, and ESFP), are characterized by Action and Freedom. SPs

are essentially impulsive; *doing* is their thing, and they must be free to act in the present, using resources, utilizing tools, and enjoying people at once. When they feel constricted, SPs become restless and feel the need to move on. Socially, they tend to be charming and witty conversationalists. SPs bring to work and to play a sense of excitement, adventure, even risk. They thrive on uncertainty, where the outcome is not known and where there is freedom to test the limits. Of all the styles, the SP works best in crises.

2. *Epimethean* or *SJs* (a combination of Sensing and Judging, namely ISFJ, ESFJ, ISTJ, and ESTJ), are characterized by Duty and Hope. Driven by the Boy Scout motto "Be Prepared," SJs are industrious, maintaining a storehouse of commodities for the unknown future. *Belonging* is their thing, and this belonging must be earned. Moreover, they are the givers in a relationship, not the receivers; the caretakers, not the cared for. Theirs is not a desire for independence (as with the SP); rather, it is a desire to serve. While the SP is compelled to be free and independent, the SJ is, in effect, compelled to be bound and obligated. As SJs age, tradition becomes more important. If traditional ceremonies and celebrations are nonexistent, SJs manage to establish and maintain them. As conservators, they are the foundation, cornerstone, and stabilizers of society. If insufficiently appreciated, they can become exhausted, depressed, and even ill.

3. *Promethean* or *NTs* (a combination of Intuition and Thinking, namely INTP, ENTP, INTJ, and ENTJ), are fascinated by Power, not over people, but over nature. *Improving* is their thing. The ability to understand, control, predict, and explain realities, these are the four aims of science; scratch an NT and you will find a scientist. These forms of power are but means to an end, for it is competency rather than power that is sought, the desire to improve. NTs love intelligence and related qualities such as capability, capacity, skill, and ingenuity. The most self-critical of all the styles, NTs can be perfectionists. Constantly alert to their own shortcomings, they question the credentials of others. This recalcitrance to established authorities can make them seem unusually individualist and even arrogant. Tending to be workaholics, NTs are forever learning; they enjoy developing models, exploring ideas, and building systems. They are regularly drawn to occupations that have to do with the formation and application of scientific principles. NTs tend to focus on the future, regarding the past as something dead and gone.

4. *Apollonian* or *NFs* (a combination of Intuition and Feeling, namely INFJ, ENFJ, INFP, and ENFP), are characterized by Spirit, elegantly

expressed in the search for Self. While the purposes of SPs (freedom from responsibility), SJs (storing commodities), and NTs (storing capabilities) are understood by SPs, SJs, and NTs alike, although they may not embrace them, the NF cannot really grasp the others' commitment to what seems to the NF to be false goals. For NFs, *becoming* is their thing. While the SPs, SJs, and NTs can go after their goals directly and full bore, the NFs search for self is circular and perpetual. Hamlet, you might recall, wrestled with this dilemma: "To be or not to be, that is the question." Seeking to satisfy their longing for unity and uniqueness, NFs hunger for self-actualization. NFs can become disenchanted, moving from cause to cause in their search for meaning. They tend to choose the humanities and the social sciences as areas of interest. Passionate in pursuit of a creative effort, NFs can be dilettantes compared to NTs, flitting from idea to idea like intellectual butterflies. They are not content with abstractions but rather seek relationships. Their quest culminates not with action but with interaction.

The following chart helps to put the contributions of temperament and personality typology in perspective. Kiersey's four temperaments are placed at the top for reference.

Kiersey's Four Temperaments	SP	SJ	NT	NF
Four Elements	Air	Soil	Water	Fire
Four Seasons	Spring	Autumn	Winter	Summer
Hindu Yogas (Religious Paths)	Karma Yoga (Path of Action)	Bhakti Yoga (Path of Devotion)	Jnana Yoga (Path of Knowledge)	Raja Yoga (Path of Liberation)
Plato's Roles	Artisan	Guardian	Rationalist	Idealist
Aristotle's Sources of Happiness	Sensuality	Property	Rationality	Morality

Kiersey's Four Temperaments	SP	SJ	NT	NF
Ezekiel's Living Creatures	Ox (hard-working)	Lion (courageous)	Eagle (far-seeing)	Human (compassionate)
The Four Gospels	Luke (service-oriented)	Mark (action-oriented)	John (symbolic)	Matthew (people-centered)
Hippocrates's Four Humors	Blood (cheerful)	Black Bile (somber)	Phlegm (calm)	Yellow Bile (enthusiastic)
Galen's Four Temperaments	Sanguine	Melancholic	Phlegmatic	Choleric
Irenaeus's Four Temperaments	Spontaneous	Historical	Scholarly	Spiritual
Adickes's Four World Views	Innovative	Traditional	Skeptical	Doctrinaire
Spränger's Four Value Attitudes	Artistic	Economic	Theoretic	Religious
Ktretschmer's Character Styles	Hypomanic	Depressive	Anesthetic	Hyperesthetic
Fromm's Four Orientations	Exploitative	Hoarding	Marketing	Receptive

The Enneagram

The Enneagram represents an approach to personality that concerns itself with normal and high-functioning behavior, and it condenses a great deal of psychological insight into a compact system that is relatively easy to understand. The term "Enneagram" was introduced by George Gurdjieff

(1879–1949), an eccentric Russian who traveled widely, particularly to Mount Athos, a rugged and isolated peninsula in Greece that is home to twenty Orthodox monasteries. There he learned esoteric practices helpful in opening human consciousness. He taught these practices to his study groups in St. Petersburg and Moscow in 1916. Gurdjieff called his system of principles of inner growth The Fourth Way, claiming it transcended the three traditional spiritual paths of the monk, the yogi, and the fakir. He taught that it is possible to live The Fourth Way while active in the world, rather than detached from life in an isolated community of like-minded seekers.

The origins of the Enneagram are uncertain, though parallels have been found in the Jewish Tree of Life (Kabbalah), the Muslim Sufi tradition, the Hindu yogic chakra tradition, and in the Christian monastic tradition of the Orthodox Church, particularly as articulated by the fourth-century Orthodox theologian Evagrius of Pontus (c. 348–399), a desert monk who taught his followers yogic techniques of concentration, including identifying psychological patterns that keep human beings locked in inner turmoil. Evagrius and other Desert Elders were familiar with Greek philosophy, particularly with Plato, who taught that the material world was a reflection of a spiritual world. Plato also quoted Pythagoras as saying, "All the world can be explained by the numbers one through nine."

The word Enneagram stems from the Greek *ennea*, meaning "nine," and *grammos*, meaning "points." The Enneagram refers to "a nine-pointed star diagram that can be used to map the process of any event from its inception through all the stages of that event's progress in the material world."[5] The Enneagram's value is in its ease of use, rooted in a time-tested tradition of understanding human nature—how it is formed, broken, and healed. The Enneagram types persons into one of nine boxes (the Perfectionist, the Giver, the Performer, the Tragic Romantic, the Observer, the Devil's Advocate, the Epicure, the Boss, and the Mediator), providing information about the way that individuals are likely to behave and therefore to get along. While lessening the tension of having to live with the mystery of the unknown, the Enneagram is not a fixed system. It is a model of interconnecting lines that indicate a dynamic movement, in which each of us has the potentials of all nine types, or points, although we identify most strongly with the issues of our own type. Interconnecting lines indicate the versatility of movement available to the individual, as well as specific relationships between the different types of individuals.

5. Palmer, *The Enneagram*, 10.

Part I – Developing a "Rule of Life"

Underlying the Enneagram is a distinction between one's essential nature and one's acquired personality. Essential nature is described as "hard wired" or what is "one's own," the potential with which we were born, rather than the personality we have acquired through education, the influence of authority figures, beliefs, and personal ideas. The Enneagram's nine-pointed star suggests that there are nine major aspects of essential being and that each may be approached in different ways. The search for a particular aspect of essence is motivated by the suffering caused by its absence. For example, if you are chronically afraid, then you have suffered the loss of the child's essential trust, whether in the environment or in others. Therefore searching for courage becomes a motive in your life.

The realization that we are acting contrary to our essential nature indicates the presence of an inner observer. The Enneagram system encourages the practice of self-observation, whereby individuals focus their attention inwardly in order to recognize habitual patterns within their minds. The fact that one can observe and talk about one's own habits of thinking and feeling from the point of view of a detached observer helps to make these habits less compulsive and automatic.

According to Gurdjieff, self-recognition of type is hindered by the presence of "buffers," psychological defense mechanisms that hide our negative traits of character from ourselves, blinding us to the forces that are at work within our own personality. The major defense mechanisms that are related to Enneagram types One through Nine, respectively, are "reaction formation, repression, identification, introjection, isolation, projection, rationalization, denial, and narcotization."[6] Gurdjieff asked his students to search inwardly for their own unconscious systems of defense.

In her book on the Enneagram, Helen Palmer identifies nine chief features (passions) of the emotional life (anger, pride, deceit, envy, greed, fear, gluttony, lust, and sloth). These emotional patterns are part of one's emotional shadow or the acquired personality, stemming from the need to cope with early family life. If a child develops in a healthy manner, then the passions are akin to mere tendencies, which can be identified with relative ease and dealt with accordingly. But if the psychological situation is severe, then one of the shadow issues becomes an obsessional preoccupation. In this case the capacity for self-observation weakens and the individual cannot move on to other things. The hope is that by identifying one's own Chief Feature, one can observe the many ways in which this habit has

---

6. Ibid., 15.

gained control over one's life. In this case, one's Chief Feature (one's passion), a neurotic habit that developed during childhood, can also become a personal mentor.

Gestalt Perspective

Trained as a classical Freudian psychoanalyst, psychiatrist Fritz Perls (1893–1970) discovered a unique approach to healing and growth that he called Gestalt Therapy. He believed that an innate growth process lies within each person, and that this inner process actively directs people toward greater health and wholeness. The Gestalt guide is there simply as a coach, seeking to aid patients to embrace the urge within toward growth and healing. Perls's work to expand a patient's awareness of the present moment led to significant psychological growth and individual healing, bypassing years of talk therapy.

In her book, *Consenting to Grace* (2006), Tilda Norberg introduces techniques associated with Gestalt Pastoral Care, an approach to caregiving that pays particular attention to another person's way of perceiving the world. Gestalt therapists are encouraged to appreciate their client's "spin" on the world without judging or controlling the unique ways individuals perceive the world. Unlike Perls, Norberg integrates Gestalt therapy with Christian spirituality, finding in that spirituality the perfect complement to the mind, body, and inner psychic dynamics with which Perls worked.

Gestalt Pastoral ministers, as taught by Norberg and other trainers, are on their own journey to healing. Practicing contemplation and allowing God's love to flow through them, Gestalt ministers seek to enter the world of the persons they are guiding, knowing that people use a particular sensory channel as their primary mode of interacting with the world. According to Norberg, there are four basic modes of perception that people use to receive input from their environment and to act within their world. These perceptual modes also affect the way people imagine, remember, and pray:[7]

1. *Visual*: most people visualize and perceive the world through their eyes. They tend to form mental pictures, even when thinking abstract thoughts. They understand and remember by forming picture-like images in their mind. When they pray they often form mental images, and when they recall they do so with visual detail. Even their language (they might say "I see" to express that they understand something) reflects their perceptual mode.

---

7. The following segment is adapted from Norberg, *Consenting to Grace*, 132–33.

2. *Auditory*: other people prefer to take in the world with their ears. In so doing, they may need to reflect out loud to help themselves know what they are thinking. In prayer they might even hear words from God with their inner ears, but generally without any accompanying images. In childhood memories, sounds may be vivid. Language patterns will tend to include auditory references such as "Sounds good to me" or "I hear you!"

3. *Sensate*: Sensate people are those who experience the world through bodily sensation. Their senses will enable them to recall things that accompanied the original experience. In prayer they may sense the presence of God, but without hearing or seeing anything. Sensate people often express themselves with visceral language such as "I felt sick about it" or "It just doesn't feel right."

4. *Cognitive*: Cognitive perceivers, called "thinkers," need to have rational understanding before they can take something in. They must analyze and categorize before they can change. In prayer they may get an idea or receive a revelation that transforms everything. For cognitive persons, ideas are central. Their language is laced with thinking referents such as "That makes sense to me" or "I think that's right." Whereas thinkers intellectualize to deal with feelings, non-cognitive people often use intellect to avoid dealing with feelings. It takes skill to determine whether a person is avoiding feelings or is truly a thinker.

Keep in mind that most people are comfortable with a mixture of these four modalities, but will usually prefer one over the others. Nearly all of us have the capacity to experience things in our non-preferred modalities, and we may even switch modalities from day to day. Psychologists, clergy, therapists, and other caregivers are aware they need to identify with their client's perceptual system in order to provide maximum benefit in the healing process. They also need to know their own modality in order to shift to what may be another's unfamiliar territory. Knowing our own preferences, how we receive and process information, will enable us to discern and appreciate our own uniqueness as well as that of others.

Having affirmed your personality type and discovered how temperament and type influence your perceptual and learning styles, it is time to discern in this rich diversity of spiritualities a plan for your own growth in faith, wholeness (salvation), and liberation.

CHAPTER 3

Developing a Plan that Supports Spiritual Growth

Tell me, what is it you plan to do with your one wild and precious life?
—MARY OLIVER

BY THIS POINT, YOU are either excited by the many possibilities for spiritual growth or overwhelmed by them. People who are committed to relationships and busy developing careers cannot intentionally devote their lives to the practice of spiritual discipline—nor should they. At some point, however, such people must pay close attention to what they feel most attracted to, discerning what seems most central in their lives and choosing priorities, disciplines, and a lifestyle that best nourish and undergird that core. In addition, they must establish priorities based upon a course of action that is genuinely feasible.

A good way to begin is to go back over ideas that engaged you as you read earlier chapters in this book, paying attention to points that you underlined or that caught your attention. If you practice journaling, you might examine comments over the last six months, looking for common themes or new promptings. As you contemplate your rule of life, set aside time for self-examination, asking the following questions:

- When have I been aware of God's presence, guidance, or grace this week? How did I respond?
- When have I been unaware of God's presence, guidance, or grace this week? Why?
- What habit of the heart do I need to acquire in order to live more faithfully?

Part I – Developing a "Rule of Life"

Next, analyze patterns in your life, asking yourself why you are more attracted to certain spiritual disciplines and forms of worship over others. Do these seem suited to your personality? Do they represent areas of growth you feel you need at this point in your life? Do they promise a measure of balance in your life you do not currently enjoy? Are you attracted to them for reasons that are not yet apparent?

We are often attracted to spiritual practices that seem natural to our personality. For example, introverted persons might be drawn to inward disciplines such as contemplative prayer and self-examination. Extraverts might be attracted to communal expressions of worship, hospitality, and social action that suit a more interactive nature. There is nothing wrong with choosing spiritual practices that feel congruent with your personality. They are likely to be the disciplines you engage in with the greatest consistency and satisfaction. They may not, however, be the practices that will stretch you toward the greatest growth or the ones you most need. Still, they are probably a good place to begin, especially if you lack spiritual discipline.

Perhaps you are drawn to a practice because it promises to bring greater balance to your life. To be healthy, you need to be whole. The Christian spiritual life expresses one's entire being, for spirituality is concerned with every dimension of human life, individually and communally. If you are an introvert, God may be leading you to open yourself to a communal spiritual practice, to develop the relational side of your spirituality. Otherwise, you will too easily revert into inward and private reflection and not grow. If you are an extravert, you need to look inward, paying attention to the motives and needs behind your desire to interact with others.

The following questions represent a good starting place in choosing disciplines for one's rule of life:

- What am I deeply attracted to, and why?
- Where do I feel God calling me to stretch and grow?
- What kind of balance do I need in my life?

When, after thinking about these questions, you are clear about your priorities, you need to ponder what is realistic. It is far better to commit to a single practice and stick with it than to take on five and quit altogether because you could not keep up. The spiritual life is a gradual growth in faithfulness, not a heroic achievement. Realistic commitment is an expression of humility.

Developing a Plan that Supports Spiritual Growth

If you are a parent staying at home with preschool children, you may want to try short periods of reflection on a scripture verse or repeat breath prayers throughout the day. You might find it helpful to practice a simple self-examination before bedtime, observing where you have felt God's presence in your family life and how you have responded to this grace. If you have a demanding job with long hours of work, you may wish to schedule a personal retreat several times a year for more in-depth opportunities in reading, prayer, and meditation. If you are retired, perhaps you have more freedom to choose how much time you devote to spiritual practices. A chronic illness or disability can be an opportunity or an impediment, depending on its nature and degree. At such times you can exercise a genuine ministry of intercession, including writing letters to those who would appreciate words of friendship and support.

Once you have decided on a realistic rule of life, choose one person you love and trust and share your plan with them. Ask that person to help hold you accountable in your practice. If you have a spiritual friend or decide to seek a spiritual director, this is the natural person to share your rule with. A small support group seeking spiritual growth together can be an excellent help in this regard. Spouses and other family members should know enough of your rule to be able to encourage, or at least not interfere needlessly with, your practice. One's spouse should not be the primary person holding you accountable in your spiritual life.

When you decide to become serious about developing your spirituality, it is important to seek support from your faith community. The Christian life is dangerous terrain to travel alone. We get easily discouraged when our disciplines become boring or challenging, and distraught when we do not experience the results we expected. Spiritual disciplines can also be manipulated for our own ends rather than offered as a means of God-transforming grace. Hence we need the wider community of faith to help us stay on track. That community comes to us through corporate worship, study, and service, and through the grace of individuals whose experience and wisdom can guide our own. The goal, of course, is the intent to love and serve God and others more fully. Such goals are infinitely worth the effort, confusion, and pain along the path.

Part I – Developing a "Rule of Life"

Encountering God: Direct and Indirect Experience

> Mere words have something of quicksand about them.
> Only experience is the rope that is thrown to us.
> —GEORGES BATAILLE

1. Biblical Experience of the Divine

The Christian story, found in the pages of scripture as well as in the developing Christian tradition, is a testament to the mighty deeds of God on our behalf. In the early stages of our spiritual development, these mighty deeds are acts about which we have read or heard. We know that we have benefited in some way from them, but they remain in the distant past. We make tremendous progress as Christians when we begin to understand that in some real but mysterious way we are actual participants in those sacred events. It is only when this happens that our spiritual journey, based upon the scriptures and the ensuing tradition, becomes authentic. Such is the witness of the First Letter of John: "We declare to you what was from the beginning, what we have heard, what we have seen with our own eyes, what we have looked at and touched with our hands, concerning the word of life—this life was revealed, and we have seen it and testify to it, and declare to you the eternal life that was with the Father and was revealed to us—we declare to you what we have seen and heard so that you also may have fellowship with us; and truly our fellowship is with the Father and with his Son Jesus Christ" (1 John 1:1–3).

Christians maintain that the Holy Spirit is our teacher, guiding us to a true appreciation of what God has done in history and continues to do in our lives. Only when we understand this in a personal way can we understand the meaning of the scriptures and enter fully into their world. Trust is an essential ingredient in this process. It is not possible to trust someone unless others testify to that person's love and concern. The scriptures ask us to trust in God's previously experienced goodness. The biblical story, filled with patriarchs and matriarchs, prophets and apostles, bear witness to the trustworthiness of God's promise to be with us, come what may, a promise supported by claims of unconditional love. Throughout church history, other predecessors in the faith join with contemporary witnesses in creating a vital community of faith, together attesting to the ongoing reality of

Developing a Plan that Supports Spiritual Growth

God's faithful presence in our midst. Here too the Holy Spirit plays a critical role, for it is the Spirit who whispers insistently to our hearts that God loves us, no matter what happens to challenge that conviction. Ultimately we too become prophets, witnessing to that reality in our own experience.

The experience of the absence of God, a nagging reality that affects some more than others, is a means whereby we are challenged to grow and mature. In the infancy of our faith journey, many relate to God as one who caters to their wishes—this is the "Santa Claus" God of early childhood. It is the God of the Galilean period in the life of Jesus, who works miracles and drives out demons and speaks eloquently. But this loving God, not unlike good and loving parents, does not want us to remain in the unreal, Santa Claus world of immaturity. At some point we enter the "wilderness" journey of our faith, a time of trial when we long for a glimpse of the Promised Land. This journey through periods of trial and the apparent absence of God are essential to our growth toward full maturity and total trust in God. The "prophetic" guides in our lives—friends and supporters who are never lacking in authentic communities of faith—will be indispensable at such times. The Holy Spirit accompanies us on our journey, and it would be nothing less than "resisting the Spirit" to avoid the hardships of the journey traced out for us by a loving God who seeks our ultimate happiness rather than the tenuous happiness we might presently prefer.[1]

According to Demetrius Dumm, during the Galilean period of our lives we come to that point where, in addition to being baptized with Jesus into his life and death and hearing the voice of God calling us to serve others, we participate with Jesus in our own transfiguration.[2] While Father Demetrius does not refer to "second-half-of-life" terminology, I believe the metaphor is particularly applicable. Such a transformation may occur in a sudden dramatic moment, as in the case of Jesus, but more likely over a period of time.

The evidence for this will be a gradual awareness that the most important thing in life may not be winning little victories that make sense in a secular or material world, but rather that our record of unselfish love becomes the only thing that really matters. The primary evidence for this critical discovery may well come only after we are not able to win those victories that seemed so important in our younger years.

---

1. For a deeper explanation of this reality, see Appendix C: "Walking the Wire – A Sermon."

2. Dumm, *Praying the Scriptures*, 73.

Part I – Developing a "Rule of Life"

According to Luke, Jesus' transfiguration happened "while Jesus was praying" (9:29), an image that implies letting go of the world's values, losing confidence in worldly success, and trusting in God's wisdom and promises rather than in our own wisdom and accomplishments. Ultimately, our transfiguration implies spending our lives in a way that brings blessing to others.

In John's Gospel, during the trial of Jesus, we come across one of the most profound statements in the Bible. There, Jesus tells Pilate: "For this I was born, for this I came into the world, to testify to the truth" (18:37). In this case "truth," one of John's favorite and most important words, does not refer to philosophical truth but rather to "what Jesus hears as he listens to the heartbeat of his heavenly Father. It is nothing less than God's disclosure of the meaning and purpose of our existence. From God's side, it is unconditional love; on our side, it is freedom and joy."[3]

In John's Gospel we are also exhorted to choose light over darkness, meaning not simply that we live ethically rather than unethically, but that we accept the responsibility that comes from this choice, namely to live unselfishly—something that entails the pain of self-denial as well as the joy of ultimate freedom ("If you continue in my word, you are truly my disciples, and you will know the truth, and the truth will make you free"; John 8:31–32). With the gift of freedom comes the obligation to use freedom as we see Jesus using it, namely, to love others so that they too may be free.

2. Ritual and Divine Experience

Since the great saving deeds of God seem to have occurred in the distant past, it is necessary to take note of the unique nature of these deeds that allows them to be reenacted at any moment in time. The reason they can remain dated in history and still vibrant today is the participation in them of a God whose nature is timeless and whose presence in any historical event always gives that event an eternal and timeless dimension. The classical way to connect these religious events to future periods of history is through the use of ritual. For Judaism, the supreme ritual moment is the Passover, for Roman Catholics the Eucharist, for Eastern Orthodoxy the liturgy, and Protestants the Word of God, read and proclaimed.

On the eve of his death, Jesus invited his disciples to participate in a ceremony called the Eucharist, or Holy Communion. The traditional understanding of this event is that Jesus used this ritual to establish his church,

3. Ibid., 78.

"ordaining" his disciples as its priests and apostles. In fact, such an interpretation could not be farther from his intention. Whatever Jesus had in mind, founding a church was not a consideration. What was on his mind, viewed spiritually, was more powerful, insightful, and relevant than establishing a "memorial meal" or instituting a ritual proclaiming his death (that is Paul's theology; see 1 Cor. 11:25–26). A passage from the Gospel of Thomas most clearly approximates what Jesus had in mind at the Last Supper: "Whoever drinks what flows from my mouth will become as I am, and I will become as he is, so that what is hidden may be manifest" (logion 108). Jesus By establishing a living channel that would allow him to remain in communion with his beloved ones, Jesus would become a life growing within their own lives. Through his continued presence in their innermost beings, they, too, would become one with him, as he stated in his closing prayer: "I in them and you in me, that they may become completely one" (John 17:23).

For Jesus and the early Christians, the bread and wine became an instantiation (a specific instance) of his own resurrection body. "Through their intentional participation in this spiritual practice, the disciples could continue to 'ingest' [Jesus'] energetic presence, and he could continue to teach them from 'inside their own skins,' at a subtle energetic level."[4] When the bread and wine are seen as an instantiation—rather than either a consubstantiation or transubstantiation[5]—of the mystical body of Christ, we step through these into the unitive experience of interabiding love, meeting Jesus "face to face." Both our own eternal reality and his are never again in question.

To those who question the reality of the presence of Jesus in the Eucharist, Father Demetrius points to the error in viewing the Eucharist as *either* real *or* symbolic, for it should be seen as real *and* symbolic. The word "symbol," which comes from the Greek, conveys the idea of bringing together two pieces so that the resulting union has a significance that neither part possesses by itself. The word "symbol," then is not opposed to what is real; rather, it is opposed to what is meaningless. When one affirms the "real" presence of Jesus in the Eucharist, the proper response is adoration; when one affirms the symbolic presence, the proper response is to affirm

---

4. Bourgeault, *Wisdom Jesus*, 186.

5. Consubstantiation is a Protestant interpretation in which Jesus becomes present with and to believers through the Eucharist; transubstantiation is the traditional Roman Catholic position in which the bread and wine are literally changed into the body and blood of Christ.

the meaning of Jesus' presence in our lives, which is to live unselfishly, embracing unselfish behavior.

When Jews participate in the Passover, they are challenged to trust in the God of the Exodus, who intervened on behalf of the Israelite slaves and who promises to continue to liberate observant Jews, feeding them with the blessings of covenant- and Torah-faithfulness. When Christians participate in the new Exodus (the Eucharist), they are challenged to abandon self-security and to undertake, with Jesus, the difficult journey into the "wilderness" of concern for others. It is a wilderness because we don't know where it will lead us. "As soon as we pledge ourselves to a life of sensitivity to the needs of others, we are led into an ever more mysterious and uncontrollable world—but also into a world that ends with a 'land flowing with milk and honey' (Num. 14:8)."[6]

Every act of unselfish love mans a little bit of dying to self in order to live for others. And when one's lifetime is filled with these little "deaths," there will be no problem dealing with the physical death that comes at the end of life.

3. Scripture and Divine Experience

For many Christians, reading scripture is an act of duty or devotion. They read it to learn content, and to be reassured of the doctrines and beliefs that shape their religious way of life. There are, of course, many ways of "reading" the Bible. The earliest and still perhaps the most complete method is called Lectio Divina. This Latin phrase means literally "divine reading," though it is better translated as "sacred reading." Originally this approach discerned four stages in the process of reading the biblical text: (1) reading (*lectio*); (2) meditation (*meditatio*); prayer (*oratio*); and contemplation (*contemplatio*). Those who utilize this approach today emphasize a meditative approach, with the intention of learning what God has to say to us about the true meaning of life for ourselves and for the world. In this prayerful reading, it is God who is being sought and the sacred text is simply the medium through which we trust that God will reveal himself to us. This searching is not the quest of a theologian to know more about God and about sacred history, though that is a noble aspiration. Rather it is a yearning to experience God's goodness and purposes in one's life. It seeks to "know" God in the biblical sense of intuitive appreciation of God's reality and divine presence.[7]

---

6. Dumm, *Praying the Scriptures*, 88.

7. For additional information on the practice of Lectio Divina, consult Appendix B.

Developing a Plan that Supports Spiritual Growth

We find an apt example of this mode of searching in a passage from John's Gospel, where two of John the Baptist's disciples begin to follow Jesus (1:35–39). The brief conversation between Jesus and the two disciples moves on two levels. Jesus turns to the disciples and asks, "What are you looking for?" This is a natural question if two people are following you. At a deeper level, of course, it is one of the great existential questions of life: "What are you searching for?" The two disciples respond, apparently naively, "Rabbi, where are you staying?" In the Greek, the word for "to stay" is also translated "to abide," which bring out an important theme in John. In 14:2 Jesus will tell the disciples that he is going to prepare "abiding places" for them, and in 14:23 he indicates that he and the Father will come to them and abide with them ("make our home with them"). In 15:2, when Jesus defines discipleship as "abiding in him as he abides in us," he uses the analogy of the vine and the branches, stating that those who abide in him will bear much fruit (15:5). The fruit, of course, is the increase of love for others. Where one stays in John's Gospel is not a reference to a location but, in the deepest sense, to one's true home in the Father's love. That is the home for which we are yearning, whether we know it or not, and it is that home to which Jesus leads us. On one level, Jesus' answer to the two disciples is a word of invitation: "come and see." But on a deeper level, we understand that this is an invitation to discipleship.

I have chosen this relatively brief episode in the ministry of Jesus to show, first of all, that Lectio Divina implies an unhurried, attentive reading of the text, which is not concerned primarily about learning something but that seeks to enter into a personal and experiential relationship with Jesus. John's Gospel is particularly insistent on the importance of a personal experience of God, in Jesus, and with the aid of the Holy Spirit.

A related approach, which follows the fourth (*contemplatio*) stage of the *lectio*, is associated with Ignatius Loyola (c. 1491–1556), the founder of the Society of Jesus (Jesuits) and author of the *Spiritual Exercises*. Loyola developed a technique of imaginative engagement in which readers of a biblical passage project themselves into the biblical narrative, viewing and experiencing it from within. Readers are encouraged to use their imagination to make themselves characters in the story, constructing a vivid and realistic mental image of the biblical scene, along with a prayerful engagement with the text. If the contemplation is on the resurrection, for example, we are to pray for joy, rejoicing with the risen Christ; if it is on the passion, we are to pray for pain and tears, suffering with Christ.

Part I – Developing a "Rule of Life"

The Ignatian retreat, a four-week program for personal and spiritual renewal, has become a well-established feature of modern Christian life, especially within Catholicism. The most characteristic features of this retreat, as specified in the *Spiritual Exercises*, can be summarized as follows: (1) an imaginative approach to the reading of scripture and prayer, in which those who undertake the exercises form mental images as aids to prayer and contemplation; (2) a structured and progressive program of reflection and meditation, which proceeds sequentially through the major themes of the Christian life. The four weeks course focuses on sin and its consequences; the life of Christ; the death of Christ; and the resurrection; (3) the use of a retreat director, who guides the practitioners through the exercises, allowing reflection on both God and self, encouraging decisions for personal reform and renewal.

4. The Ultimate Experience of the Divine

Corporately and individually, rituals are important as means to an end, which is personal union with God. As ends, religious rites can easily become a form of idolatry. The answer to this dilemma is not to eliminate rituals, for we are communal creatures, but to remember that the fruit of personal experience with God must always be found in our love and service toward others. As the biblical Job discovered, rituals can be dead ends, particularly when personal encounter is the goal: "I had heard of you by the hearing of the ear [knowing through ritual], but now my eye sees you [knowing through encounter]" (Job 42:5).

When we read the story of the cure of a man born blind in John 9, we notice that there is a clear progression in his gaining sight. The restoration of his physical sight was only the beginning of his cure; he begins to acquire spiritual sight only when, in response to a question about who had given him his sight, he is able to say that "the man called Jesus" had done it (9:11). He is gaining spiritual sight, but his faith is still inadequate since it depends upon the witness of others. The man moves toward greater clarity in stages until the culmination at the end of the story, when he declares that he believes in Jesus and proceeds to worship him (9:38). Only at this point has the blind man been fully and finally cured.

Mary Magdalene's experience at the resurrection of Jesus provides another example. In Luke's version, the angels inform Mary Magdalene and the other women the good news of the resurrection, so that when they inform the male disciples, their witness is indirect. In John's Gospel, Mary comes to know about the resurrection—the most important discovery in her life—directly, through a personal encounter with the risen Christ, who is now viewed as a dear friend (20:11–18).

Words and rituals are indispensable for us humans, who rely greatly on signs, symbols, and other pointers to the divine, and we will never reach the point of not needing them. However, religious words and acts are not ends in themselves but are intended to bring us to a transformational relationship with God that is profoundly personal and experiential. According to William Blake, "All we need to do is cleanse the doors of perception, and we shall see things as they are—eternal."[8] We should never settle for anything less than this experience.

It is through the radical Jesus of the gospels as well as through the Holy Spirit that we touch God not as a concept but as a living reality. According to Zen master Thich Nhat Hanh, the beloved Vietnamese monk who for decades has lived in dialogue with Christianity, every human has the seed of the Spirit within them, meaning that each person has the capacity of healing, transforming, and loving. Through mindfulness—focusing deeply on the present moment—human beings can touch that seed and therefore touch God the Father and God the Son.[9] While Hanh has a deep respect for concepts, he views them as means, not as ends. Gently but firmly, he leads others from theory to practice, from concept to experience. Buddhism does not focus on faith but on practice. For example, Buddhists do not focus on nirvana, because nirvana means the extinction of all notions, concepts, and speech. Instead, Buddhists practice mindfulness, through sitting meditation, walking meditation, mindful eating, and so on. "Living mindfully, shining the light of our awareness on everything we do [is how] we touch the Buddha, and our mindfulness grows."[10] According to Hanh, "the living Christ" is present when Christians manifest Jesus by their way of life. When the church manifests understanding, tolerance, and loving-kindness, Jesus is there. In Buddhism, as in Christianity, practicing the teaching is the highest form of prayer.

This form of living, called "nondualistic thinking" by Buddhists and "contemplation" by Christian mystics, will teach us how to actually experience our experiences, whether good, bad, or ugly, and how to let them transform us. The dualist mind gives us sanity and safety, and that is good

---

8. Cited in Rohr, *Naked Now*, 85.
9. Hanh, *Living Buddha, Living Christ*, 15.
10. Ibid., 21–22.

enough for survival. But to address our social and religious problems in any creative and final way, we need something more, something bigger, better, and more profound. We need a new mind, "the mind of Christ" (1 Cor. 2:16). Non-polarity thinking teaches us how to hold creative tensions, how to live with paradox and contradiction, how to embrace mystery, and therefore how to actually practice what all religions teach as necessary: compassion, mercy, patience, forgiveness, and humility. This is transformative religion. As Richard Rohr puts it: "When you can be present, you will know the Real Presence. I promise you this is true."[11]

In John's Gospel, as Jesus prepares his disciples for his passion, he gives them a new commandment: "Just as I have loved you, you also should love one another" (13:34). At first glance, it appears that Jesus is asking them to imitate his loving, which they are unable to observe, but in fact he is asking them to receive a gift. By receiving this gift, which is love, they are recreated to share the very life of God. It is in this sense that Jesus' commandment sums up all previous ones. It is old (Lev. 19:18) yet it is also new in that it models the self-giving love of Christ and of God. The "new" aspect of this commandment is that those who belong to Jesus are asked to enter into the love that denotes the relationship of the Father and the Son. The demonstration of that love will be the primary witness to the world that they are Jesus' disciples.

It has taken me a long time to appreciate the profundity of Christianity's clearest teaching: that *when disciples live in love, they experience God*, who is Love. This love is possible when you understand that on some essential level all things are connected. This understanding cannot be merely intellectual. It must be experiential, the insight gained by deep touching and deep looking in a daily life of prayer, contemplation, and meditation. Experience teaches that the best way to love God is by taking good care of ourselves, all living beings, and the environment. In this way we discover the truth underlying all experience of the divine: the unity and interdependence of all things.

---

11. Rohr, *Naked Now*, 12.

Part II – The First Half of Life

CHAPTER 4

Essential Tasks for the First-Half Journey

> Learn and obey the rules very well,
> so you will know how to break them properly.
> —THE DALAI LAMA

THE TASK OF THE first half of life, according to Richard Rohr, is to build a strong "container" or identity. This task addresses three essential questions: (1) what makes me significant? (2) how can I support myself? and (3) who will go with me? The first half of life, however, is not the full journey. It is only the starting gate. The task of the second half is to find the actual contents that this container was meant to hold and deliver. Both halves are cumulative and sequential, and both are necessary. To quote Archimedes, you must have both "a lever and a place to stand" before you can move the world. The realization that there is a further journey should lead us to consider the first half journey as a warm-up rather than as the adventure itself, as preparation rather than as destination.

The concerns of the first half of life are vital and instrumental to the further journey and could be accomplished much more effectively if they were viewed in tandem with what follows. In fact, if one realized that there was a further journey, one might do the warm-up quite differently. For most people, the concerns of the first half of life involve six interrelated tasks, all focused around survival:

1. Establishing one's personal identity;
2. Creating boundary markers;
3. Seeking security;
4. Finding mentors;

5. Committing to significant people and projects; and
6. Securing one's lifestyle and career.

There has probably never been a culture in human history that did not value law, tradition, custom, authority, boundaries, and a clear sense of morality.¹ Such containers provide humans with the requisite security, continuity, predictability, impulse control, and ego structure needed to confront the challenges of life. Individuals grounded in these foundations tend to grow up more naturally and happily than those who receive little by way of guidance. Without boundaries, but also without pushing against those boundaries, humans cannot develop fully or naturally. Required behavior and beliefs are good and necessary to get us started. But when we invest in them too heavily, they soon hold us back. As Paul says, they are like a disciplinarian ("custodian," RSV; "tutor," KJV; Gal. 3:24) to help us get started. Like training wheels on a bicycle, they keep us safe and prevent us from falling. But if we rely on them too long, we never "grow up."

Ironically, one needs a strong ego structure to let go of ego; one cannot or should not give up a self that is not well formed. As two-year-olds assert their identity and teenagers their rebellion, so we find in nature that goslings must break their shells and butterflies their cocoons in order to fly. The creature cannot be healthy and whole unless its egg shell is tough and its cocoon resistant. But if one remains in the protected half of life beyond its natural period, one becomes a "well-disguised narcissist or an adult infant (who is also a narcissist)—both of whom are often thought to be successful 'good old boys' by the mainstream culture."²

Buddhists speak of "the hungry ghost," by which they mean a stage of humanity. The more one eats (the greater the materialistic urge), the hungrier one gets. Trying to fill the hole within with food, money, power, or the admiration of others only deepens the hole. The Hungry Ghost is considered the worst of lives.

In the New Testament, the calls of Jesus to potential followers consist generally of invitations to leave family, home, and careers for a second journey (Matt. 4:22; Luke 14:26). When Jesus called his first disciples, he was inviting people to further journeys who were already socially and religiously settled. He was not talking about joining a new security system or a religious denomination. In some cases, however, he recognized that some

1. The following segment is adapted from chapter 3 of Rohr, *Falling Upward*, 25–43.
2. Ibid., 26–27.

could not answer a second call because they had not yet completed the first task (Luke 14:28–30). Unless you build your first house well, you will never leave it. Abraham did a lot of "possessing," Jacob a lot of conniving, David a lot of killing, and Paul a lot of persecuting before being ready to go to the next stage of the journey. "To build your house well is ironically to be nudged beyond its doors."[3]

Most of us cannot move ahead because we have not completed the first task or learned from previous ones. According to Bill Plotkin, most individuals remain forever stymied in the adolescent phase, unable to move to ensuing phases of life.[4] They were either unable to build their first "house" well, or not at all. They can—and will—move forward as soon as they have completed and lived the previous stage. The process cannot be rushed. When the time is right, when the old agenda becomes insufficient or falls apart, they will almost naturally fall forward, no longer needing the previous stage.

Before we describe living in the upper story of our house, let us address in greater detail how we build the foundation. To some extent, the process involves trial and error. In order to learn how to ride a bicycle, one must learn how to fall, and how to recover from falling. It is precisely by falling that one learns balance. Surfers, skiers, skaters, all must learn to push both right and left in order to gain confidence, dexterity, and a sense of direction. But without some degree of order, predictability, and technique, competence remains beyond reach. Children need limits to their freedom and emotions if they are to be teachable. Without laws like the Ten Commandments, human existence would be chaotic, vicious, and violent.

The secret to mature adulthood and self-control is for children to learn through trial and error in an environment whereby parents and other early authority figures provide a combination of unconditional love together with conditional and demanding love.[5] Both law and freedom are necessary for spiritual growth, as Paul says in Romans and Galatians. He learned this from Jesus, who repeated six times the expression "the Law says . . . but I say" (Matt. 7:21–48), while assuring us that he "has not come to abolish the law or the prophets" but to bring them to completion (5:17). The most effective organizations are said to have both a "good boss" and a "bad boss," who work closely together. One leader maintains allegiance, while

---

3. Ibid., 23.
4. Plotkin, *Nature and the Human Soul*, 5–6.
5. Fromm, *Art of Loving*, 43–44.

the other sets clear goals and limits. As the apostle Paul states in his letter to the Romans: "if it had not been for the law [Torah], I would not have known sin. I would not have known what it is to covet if the law had not said, 'You shall not covet'" (7:7). The Bible contains clear passages describing God's conditional love and covenant expectation, but it also describes God's unconditional love, giving it the final word.

While people in some cultures accomplish the first-half process much better, few monotheists (Jews, Christians, and Muslims) have been taught how to live both law and freedom at the same time. Our Western dualistic minds do not process paradoxes very well. Without an imaginative and contemplative mind, we do not know how to hold creative tensions. We are better at rushing to judgment and demanding complete resolution to situations before we have learned what they have to teach us. There is evidence that many traditional (primal) societies produced healthy psyches and ego structures by doing the first half of life well, even if they were not as "developed" or individuated as we are. Indigenous people in undeveloped cultures in India, the Philippines, and Latin America often seem much less neurotic and anxious than we are, and can deal with failure or loss far more easily than we can. For that reason "developed" societies seldom produce elders, wise people concerned less with themselves and more with the wellbeing of neighborhoods, societies, and the planet. Having successfully navigated their first-half journeys, elders have learned not to arrive at answers too quickly, avoiding the scary fundamentalist thinking found in corporations, institutions, and in all of the world religions. Most wars, genocides, and tragedies in history have been waged by unquestioning followers of dominating leaders. Humans love the familiar, the habitual, their own groups, and they are all tied deeply to their early conditioning, even if it means following leaders and ideologies that lead us to do evil. Such behavior frees us from the burden of thinking and critiquing and from personal responsibility. Thus the gospel call, again and again, is to leave home, family, and nets (Mark 1:16–20). Without that necessary separation, order itself—our particular kind of order—will often feel like a form of "salvation." It has been the most common and counterfeit substitute for the real liberation offered by mature religion.

The solution, at least in the first half of life, is not to choose between law and freedom, but to embrace them symbiotically. Our generation is perhaps the first generation in history to have the freedom both to know the rules and also to critique them at the same time. Unfortunately, those who have not been able to do the task of the first journey well often go back and try to do it again, often overdoing it. This pattern is usually an inconsistent mix of old-fashioned styles and symbols with contemporary ideologies of consumerism, technology, militarism, and individualism. The result is a form of perpetual adolescence, characterized by inability to let go and embrace the second-half-of-life journey.

The Loyal Soldier[6]

Bill Plotkin's work with the Animas Institute in Durango, Colorado, offers a specific plan for moving from what he calls an "egocentric" worldview to a "soulcentric" one.[7] Saddened by how much of our world stays at the egocentric first stage of life, Plotkin utilizes an illustration from post-World War II Japan that demonstrates how returning soldiers could be helped to move from their identity as "loyal soldiers" to rejoin their communities as useful citizens.[8] During their formative years, their only identity had been to be a loyal soldier to their country. They needed a broader identity that would help them move from the identity of the first half of life to growth in the broader identity of the second half of life.

So certain Japanese communities created a communal ritual whereby soldiers were publicly thanked and praised for their service to the people. After this an elder would stand and announce with authority that the war was now over and that the community needed them to let go of what had served them well up till then. The final charge went something like this: "The community needs you to return as a man, a citizen, and something beyond a soldier."

This kind of closure is much needed for most of us at the end of all major transitions in life, particularly to the second half of our lives. The Japanese created clear closure, transition, and possible direction. Most people in the West have no clear sense of crossover. We are not shown the stunted and limited character of the worldview of the first half of life, so we simply continue with more of the same. Even in the church there is little talk of journeys outward or onward, the kind of journeys to which Jesus called his followers. The state too wants loyal patriots and citizens, not thinkers, critics, or citizens of a larger world. No wonder we have so much depression

---

6. This segment is adapted from Rohr, *Falling Upward*, 43–51.
7. Plotkin, *Nature and the Human Soul*, 3.
8. Plotkin, *Soulcraft*, 91–92; *Wild Mind*, 129–131.

and addiction, especially among the elderly but also among the churched. "Their full life has been truncated with the full cooperation of both church and state."[9] While such a view might sound extreme, from a second-half perspective it is accurate.

The loyal soldier is similar to the "elder son" in Jesus' parable of the prodigal son. His very loyalty to strict meritocracy, to his own entitlement, to obedience and loyalty to his father, keeps him from the very "celebration" that same father prepares, and to which he begs the son come (Luke 15:25–32). We have no indication the elder son ever came to the feast. What a judgment on first-stage religion. Jesus makes the same point in his story of the Pharisee and the tax collector (Luke 18:9–14), in which one is loyal and observant and deemed wrong, whereas the one who has not obeyed the law is justified. Both the elder son and the Pharisee are good loyal religious soldiers, exactly what most of us in the church have been told to be, yet Jesus states that both missed the major point.

The loyal soldier is needed, helping us through the first half of life safely, teaching us to look both ways before we cross the street, to have enough impulse control to avoid addictions and compulsive emotions, to learn the sacred "No" to ourselves that gives us dignity, identity, direction, significance, and boundaries. We must learn these lessons well to get off to a good start.[10] It is far easier to begin life with a conservative worldview and respect for tradition than with little or no respect for tradition. But many just fall in love with this initial sense, see it as an extension of themselves, and spend their who life building a white picket fence around it.

Without our loyal soldier protecting us in the first half of life, many of us would succumb to addiction, promiscuity, ego, and vanity. Rootless and aimless, we would have no home base and no sustained relationships. We would have lots of levers, but no place to stand. Paradoxically, our loyal soldier gives us so much security and validation that his voice is often confused with the voice of God. The loyal soldier is the voice of all our early authority figures, masculine and feminine alike, but it is not the "still, small voice" of God (1 Kgs. 19:13) that gives us power instead of eviscerating it.

The loyal soldier can get us through a lot, especially with the early decisions that demand black-and-white thinking, but it cannot get you to the second half of life. The loyal soldier helps us win the battles of the first

---

9. Rohr, *Falling Upward*, 45.

10. Plotkin discusses Loyal Soldier subpersonalities and survival strategies in *Wild Mind*, 128–52.

journey, but in the second journey the loyal soldier always loses, because he is invariably fighting God. "The first battles solidify the ego and create a stalwart loyal soldier; the second battles defeat the ego because God always wins. No wonder so few want to let go of their loyal soldier; no wonder so few have the faith to grow up. The ego hates losing, even to God."[11]

According to Rohr, the loyal soldier is similar to what Freud called the superego, which usually substitutes for any real adult formation of conscience. The superego masquerades as God, because people have had nothing else to guide them, but such a conscience is a terrible substitute for authentic morality. Instead of always trying to change the circumstances or other people, the loyal soldier's ineffective character is revealed in its opposition to change and growth, and in its substituting of minor moral issues for the larger ones that ask us to change. Jesus called it "straining out gnats while swallowing camels" (Matt. 23:24).

There is a deeper voice of God, which one must learn to hear and obey in the second half of life. It will sound a great deal like the voices of risk, trust, surrender, love, and soul, coming from your deepest self. The true faith journey only begins at this point. Up to now everything is mere preparation. Finally, we have a container strong enough to hold the contents of our real life, which is filled with contradictions, paradoxes, adventures, and immense challenges. Wholeness and holiness will always stretch us beyond our comfort zones. How could they not?

So God, life, and destiny must loosen the loyal soldier's grasp on our soul, which up to now has felt like the only "I" that you know and the only authority that exists. Rohr suggests that our loyal soldier normally begins to be discharged somewhere between the ages of thirty-five and fifty-five, if it happens at all, but my experience suggests it can begin earlier, as it did for my wife Susan in her early twenties and for some of my students in their late teens, and as late as one's retirement.

To let go of one's loyal soldier is severe and painful, like the experience of loss, exile, even of death. Normally we will not discharge our loyal soldier until he shows himself to be inadequate for the real issues of life, as when we confront love, death, suffering, subtlety, and mystery. It is another form of the falling and dying that the world mythologies keep talking about, or about the "baptism into Christ's death" spoken of by the apostle Paul (Rom. 6:3–4). No one oversees his or her own demise willingly, even when it is the false self that is dying. St. John of the Cross spoke of God's work in the

---

11. Rohr, *Falling Upward*, 47.

soul as "in secret" and "in darkness," because if we fully knew what was happening, we would either try to take charge or stop the process. When we first discharge our loyal soldier, it may feel like a loss of faith or loss of self, but it is only the death of the false self and often the very birth of the soul. Perhaps the best word for this process—as for God—is Mystery. "We move forward in ways that we do not even understand and through the quiet workings of time and grace. When we get there, we are never sure just how it happened, and God does not seem to care who gets the credit, as long as our growth continues.[12] As St. Gregory of Nyssa said in the fourth century, "Sin happens whenever we refuse to keep growing."

The Journey Motif in Scripture: The Example of Abraham

In the Bible, the prototypical model for the journey of faith is found in the patriarchal stories of Genesis 12–50, starting with the story of Abraham. At some point it becomes evident that the underlying significance of this account is not the stories of the patriarchs but the story of Israel's self-understanding. When this material was put into writing, the main question was not, "Who are Abraham, Isaac, Jacob, and Joseph?" but "Who is Israel?" Israel was grappling with her self-understanding as a people called by God. The answer to that metaquestion is given in the portrayal of Abraham, Isaac, and Jacob, patriarchs whose lives were characterized by common traits:

a. They *lived by faith in God*. In Abraham, Israel understands something about herself, that she has been called into existence by God himself, that she has been created by God's initiative and preserved by God's grace. This is a dominant theme during the Babylonian Exile (see Isa. 41:8–10).

b. They are *called to be a servant people*. Election does not mean that some people are chosen because they are better than others, but rather that they are called to spread God's grace. God's purpose, as seen in Genesis 12:3, is a universal purpose, one that moves from particulars to universals, from individuals to communities and nations. In Abraham, God brings one person of faith into existence in order that God's blessing might be extended to all humanity. This is the Bible's stress on election, that when God calls a people, they are called to service, and the rest of the Old Testament, into the gospels and epistles, shows what it means to be a servant people. The Bible makes it clear that Israel's calling is part of God's healing

---

12. Ibid., 51.

intention (the biblical word for healing, health, wholeness, and goodness is "salvation," like the Hebrew word "shalom"). In the Bible, the election of a people becomes the basis for good news, what the New Testament calls "gospel." This is the message of Genesis 12–50, and it is transported to a higher key in the New Testament.

c. They are *called to a life of pilgrimage*—a life of mobility, movement, and change. Biblical faith is a calling faith, a calling to go forth, to be on the way, to be moving in God's direction, to be pioneers of faith. Abraham was told to break his ties with his land and his former security, a way of life that up to that point had been deeply rooted to the land. Like Abraham, God's people are called to nomadic consciousness. We see that clearly in the prophetic consciousness, a stance that is counter-cultural in the sense that one can be both an agent of change and a critic of the established order. The prophetic message was that God was doing a new thing. As demonstrated in Abraham's life, faith is not so much consent or agreement as something dynamic, manifested in movement. So Abraham is the ancestor of a pilgrim people, as we learn in Hebrews 11:8–12, and his story highlights the themes of mobility and change, meaning that when faith becomes lifeless, stagnant, or frozen, whether into institutions with superiority complexes or into self-serving lifestyles, God breaks them down and forces his people into radical recommitment. The story of Abraham and the patriarchs is the story of God on the move with his people.

Genesis 12:1–3 provide the theological foundation for the entire patriarchal history, for here we are given three elements that drive the narrative of faith:

1. *The command* (v. 1); "Go." This word is dynamic, setting the stage for movement, pilgrimage, and sojourning. God initiates the journey.

2. *The promise* (vv. 1–2); the patriarchs and Israel are guided by God's promise, consisting of two elements: land and posterity. In this promise Israel is given hope for the future.

3. *The blessing* (vv. 2–3); the blessing appears in three stages: (a) Abraham; (b) those who are at hand; and (c) those who are far off (all the nations and races of the world).

This passage represents one of the greatest promises of scripture, God's desire and promise to bless all the peoples and nations of the world. Here we have the basis of "faith" in the Bible, not only the trustful acceptance of God's promise but also a trust in God's faithfulness to the promise, that is, in God's ability to deliver Good News to everyone, something God accomplished through Jesus Christ and his followers, and that of course includes us. Faith, as we learn in 1 Corinthians 13, comes first in this trilogy of graces. Without faith we cannot have hope, and without hope we cannot have true, agape love.

For early Hebrews, the notion of promise was undoubtedly interpreted to mean that something would be fulfilled immediately. But as we examine the life of Abraham and the patriarchs, which represents the storyline of Israel and of all people of faith, we discover a lesson that Israel often needed to learn, and that all people of faith need to learn: that there is an interim between promise and fulfillment, and that God's people are to live in that interim by faith, trusting upon God's faithfulness.

An existential dilemma arises: How can we believe in God? How can we be sure that God will keep God's promises? How can we trust when there often seems to be so little evidence? Note Abraham's dilemma in Genesis 15:2: "O Lord God, what will you give me, for I continue childless, and the heir of my house is Eliezer of Damascus?" Genesis 12–21 depicts Abraham's first-half-of-life story, an eventful journey through the interim between promise and fulfillment. While there are hints of faith, Abraham is predominantly "walking by sight," sometimes emotionally, sometimes rationally, but generally in human and therefore in manipulative attempts to enact God's plan for his life. Proceeding cautiously, carefully, according to the misguided principles of his first-half-of-life container, Abraham proves he is not yet ready for his second-half-of-life journey. At one point there is a famine, and Abraham goes to Egypt with his family, where he deceives the Pharaoh by passing Sarah off as his sister. Abraham resorts to deception, believing this is necessary not only to protect himself and his family, but to keep God's promise alive.

The tension of the promise continues in chapter 16, with the story of Hagar and Ishmael. Mesopotamian law taught that a slave could inherit an estate in the case of childlessness. Sarah and Abraham feel they must have misunderstood God, so they take legal action, arranging for Abraham to have a son by Sarah's servant, Hagar. Once again God intervenes. Using the law to one's advantage is not what God had in mind. Ishmael was not to be the child of promise. In Genesis 17:17 we learn that the promise becomes absurd to Abraham, and he and Sarah respond with laughter and disbelief. But verse 21 repeats the promise that Sarah, who has been barren for ninety years, will bear a son. In verse 19 the author plays on the meaning of the name "Isaac," which means "he laughs."

The mystery of testing and providence continues in chapter 22. This account represents Abraham's initiation into the second half of life, his trial "by fire." The child of promise is born, but shortly thereafter, the testing of faith is taken to the limit. Isaac is the fulfillment of God's promise, but God now asks Abraham to sacrifice the only means by which the promise can be fulfilled. Abraham understands that he must trust God unconditionally, and that's when he learns that the fundamental issue at stake, not only in his life but in all of scripture, is the faithfulness of God. This is made clear in verse 14, at which point Abraham names the place of sacrifice "The Lord will provide," a dual idea of God's provision and God's providence. In letting go of his first-half-of-life values, indeed of his false ego, and in trusting God unconditionally, Abraham passes through death to a new life. The promise of Genesis 12:3 has been fulfilled; the second half of life beckons.

The Johannine Peter and the Beloved Disciple

The Gospel of John relates a fascinating account of two disciples of Jesus: Peter and an anonymous follower called "The Beloved Disciple." Peter, a model of the first half of life, is a person of many words, often pointing to self. A doer, he regularly takes charge, finding fault, living boldly, impetuously, and immaturely. He takes risks, yet denies Jesus, fearful for his life. At the end, having lived fully, he becomes a wounded healer, benefiting from his mistakes. Designated by Jesus to be shepherd of the community, he becomes an effective leader.

The Beloved Disciple, a model of the second half of life, is a person of few words, pointing beyond self. A facilitator, he remains anonymous, living faithfully, intuitively, and insightfully. Reclining next to Jesus at the Last Supper, he remains close to his Lord. In John's Gospel he is the first to arrive at the tomb, the first to believe, and the first to recognize Jesus in his post-resurrection Galilean appearance (21:7). A human paraclete (advocate, intercessor, helper, comforter), he embodies the Spirit's activity in the community and is designated by Jesus to be teacher of the community.[13]

---

13. Vande Kappelle, *Truth Revealed*, 264–70.

CHAPTER 5

The Middle Passage
(The Work of Midlife)

> No problem can be solved from the same level
> of consciousness that created it.
>
> —ALBERT EINSTEIN

THIS CHAPTER ADDRESSES WHAT some call "midlife," "the midlife transition," "the middle passage," or more dramatically "the midlife crisis." So pervasive has this phenomenon become that as we approach this time of life we almost automatically begin to brace for a psychological emergency.[1] Of course, not everyone experiences severe disruption in their middle years, and recent research shows that in all of life humans are in psychological process and therefore subject to internal flux and change. But for most people, at midlife the self goes through a transformation, "crossing-over" from one psychological identity to another. Typically, the midlife transition lasts several years and occurs somewhere between the ages of thirty-five and fifty, usually falling around the age of forty.[2]

As the midlife transition begins, whether it does so gradually or abruptly, "persons generally feel gripped by depression, feelings of disillusionment and disappointment, a sense of loss, nostalgic periods of grieving for some vaguely felt absence, a keen and growing sense of life's limits, attacks of panic about one's own death, and exercises in rationalization and denial."[3] Sometimes the reason for this sense of loss is obvious: the death of children or parents, divorce, or failure in one's career. Physically a person

1. Stein, *In Midlife*, 1.
2. Ibid., 25.
3. Ibid., 24.

may be showing signs of aging, and so earlier self-images start to shatter. It may be a time when parents are either dying or becoming dependent on their children, thus reversing earlier roles. And a person's own children may be achieving some measure of separation and independence. Quite often, however, the immediate cause is not at all clear.

The threat caused by this severe internal restructuring can produce a defensive retreat into former patterns of identity. On the other hand, this era of change can create movement into spiritual and psychological depth. According to Carl Jung, the pioneering psychiatrist who first analyzed the midlife phenomenon, a prolonged journey of this sort could lead a person to discover the core of his or her being, the Self. This discovery of the Self, and the gradual stabilization of its presence and guidance within conscious life, would become the foundation for a new experience of identity and integrity, based on an internal center rather than rooted in externals pressures from parental figures and cultural influences and expectations.[4] What one can gain from going all the way through the midlife transition, then, is the sense of an internal non-egoist Self and the feeling of integrity and wholeness that results from living in conscious contact with it. The midlife transition and crisis involve making this crucial shift from an ego-orientation to a Self-orientation, from attachment to the false self (*persona*) to the True Self.

If we reflect on the psychological purpose of the midlife transition, one result seems to be that it brings about a new kind of self-awareness, namely, consciousness of what is otherwise perhaps sensed, but only vaguely, as the tacit background of waking life, "the unconscious." In liminality (the transitional phase of a rite of passage, with its life-changing impetus) a person has the chance to realize he or she is a self, a soul, and not only a function, an ego. In Jungian terms, this is awareness of the unconscious itself, and it leads to a sense of the foundations upon which consciousness rests, the archetypal dimensions of psychological reality. Ultimately, this can lead to consciousness of a non-egoic Self that plays through all experience though previously suppressed or denied by purely egoic self-perception. "At midlife, through the experience of liminality, the soul is freed from its self-delusion and awakens to a level that endures beyond the ego's defeat and death."[5]

The optimal outcome of the midlife transition is the creation of a holistic, inclusive, and consequently more integrated sense of identity that

4. Ibid., 27.
5. Ibid., 61.

allows for the play of "floating in liminality," reminding the individual that journeying is the new norm and one's true home. Rather than fortifying one's false ego, one is now less guarded, more generous, and less protective of talents and belongings. But this is an ideal. The danger in this phase is that liminality will be excluded from spirituality due to preoccupation with the architecture of identity and consciousness that is being built during this period. New dogmatic certainties can harden to rigidity as a person leaves midlife and enters the years of mature adulthood. One of the major tasks of persons in the second half of life is to identify ways of staying effectively in touch with liminality. One way to do so is to welcome inconveniences, interruptions, mistakes, even illness and loss, all nuisances to the false ego but grist for the True Self. Another way is to focus on dreams.

Your dreams are both powerful and rebellious. They are not bound by your fears, inertia, or self-image. They don't have to be reasonable, nor do they have to please your parents, your boss, or the church. They are free to take you to interior places you can't imagine and challenge the way you run your life, or the way life runs you. They can be daring, zany, and playful. They speak truth as they point to your particular needs to growth. They highlight the changes you are able to make, but also parts of you that you have denied.[6] According to Tilda Norberg, "Whatever you have disowned in yourself shows up in your dreams. Dreams are often projections of a part of you that you don't like, are afraid of, or simply don't know about."[7] Fritz Perls called the parts that function as opposites of how one thinks of oneself "polarities"; Carl Jung called this disowned material "the shadow." Keep in mind that one's shadow includes "good" qualities as well as "bad" or "shameful" qualities that one denies. As one makes room for one's polarities, one becomes healthier and more open to transforming grace. If dreams express one's natural human spirituality, they also provide a venue in which God's presence can be discerned.

Midlife is, of course, less a chronological event than a psychological/spiritual experience. Two Greek words for "time," *chronos* and *kairos*, observe this distinction. *Chronos* is sequential, linear time; *kairos* is time revealed in its depth, a reference to the momentous, life-altering quality of time. The English language hints at this distinction by differentiating between "historical" events—those that happen in time—and "historic" events—events of importance in time. While *chronos* is quantitative, *kairos*

---

6. Norberg, *Chocolate-Covered Umbrella*, 26–27.
7. Ibid., 52.

The Middle Passage (The Work of Midlife)

has a qualitative nature. In the New Testament *kairos* means "the appointed time in the purpose of God," the time when God acts (e.g. Mark 1:15, "the *kairos* is fulfilled"). At midlife, or at crisis moments, a vertical dimension, *kairos*, intersects the horizontal plane of life, rendering a depth perspective to one's life. Midlife has as its necessary goal the righting of balance, the restoration of the person to a humble but dignified relationship to the universe, when persons go through a fundamental shift in their alignment with life and with the world, and this shift has psychological and spiritual meaning beyond the interpersonal and social dimensions. Midlife is a crisis of the spirit, when old selves are lost and new ones come into being.[8]

The midlife crisis presents us with an opportunity to reexamine our lives and to ask the liberating question, "Who am I apart from my history and the roles I have played?" When we discover that we have been living what constitutes a "false self," that we have been enacting a provisional adulthood, driven by unrealistic expectations, then "we open the possibility for the second adulthood, our true personhood."[9] Midlife is an occasion for redefining and reorienting the personality, a rite of passage between the extended adolescence of first adulthood and our inevitable encounter with old age and mortality. Those who travel the passage consciously render their lives more meaningful. Those who do not, remain prisoners of childhood, however successful they may appear in outer life. When the soul awakens at midlife and presents its gifts, life is permanently marked by the inclusion of them. Taken in, they become the hallmark of your life, the core of your uniqueness. Refused, they can haunt your days and may undermine your best efforts.

It is necessary to go through midlife to more nearly achieve one's potential and to earn the vitality and wisdom of mature aging. Thus, the midlife transition represents a summons from within to move from the provisional life to true adulthood, from the false self to authenticity. After midlife, no one can say where the journey will take them. They only know that they must accept responsibility for themselves, that the path taken by others is not necessarily for them, and that what they are ultimately seeking lies within, not out there. As the Grail legend suggested centuries ago, it is "a shameful thing to take the path others have trod." It is only from within that we perceive the prompting of the soul, and it is this emphasis on inner rather than outer truth that distinguishes the second journey from the first.

8. Stein, *In Midlife*, 3.
9. Hollis, *Middle Passage*, 7.

As Jung reminds us, "Only the person who can consciously assent to the power of the inner voice becomes a personality."[10]

In the end, we either embody some essential or our lives remain unfulfilled. Jung's central question illumines our passage through the dark midlife tunnel: "Am I related to something infinite or not?" It is, indeed, the telling question of one's life. A great mysterious energy is embodied at conception, remains awhile, and finally departs. Let us be gracious hosts, consciously assenting to the luminous midlife, the passage to the greater journey.

The Middle Passage: Theological Imagery[11]

There is no practical or compelling reason to leave one's comfort zone in life—unless we must! If you are on a spiritual journey, sooner or later you will be led to the edge of your private resources. Some event, person, idea, death, dearth, or relationship will enter your life and you will find yourself unable to cope, using your present skill set, your acquired knowledge, or your willpower. Such unwelcome events, including accidents, suffering, disappointment, and personal failure, can be life's best mentors.

On this spiritual journey, people almost always encounter a major dilemma, leaving them "wounded" in some way, and their faith story largely pivots around the resolution of the trials that result. The catalyst for the further journey is always a wounding, and the great epiphany is that the wound becomes a sacred key, a wound that changes them dramatically.

It seems a rule in the spiritual realm that we do not really find something until we first lose it—and then we must long for it, choose it, and personally claim it again, but this time on a new level. I sense this is what leads many Peace Corps volunteers, missionaries, and skilled people to leave their countries for difficult lands and challenges. Their wound, sense of longing, experience of loss, or commitment to others propels them into the further journey, either as an invitation from their soul or out of deep devotion to God. At some point we will stumble over a necessary stumbling-stone, as Isaiah calls it (Isa. 8:14); at some point we will and we must "lose" at something. There will be, and, if we are honest, there must be at least one situation in our lives that we cannot fix, control, explain, change, or even understand. This is the crucible (the vessel that holds molten metal in one place long enough to be purified and clarified), the gateway to

10. Cited by Hollis, ibid., 116.
11. This segment is adapted from Rohr, *Falling Upward*, 65–104.

transformation, forcing us to let go of egocentric preoccupations, transporting us on the further and larger journey. In the case of Francis of Assisi, the moment came when he kissed the leper. As he describes it in his *Testament*, "What before had been nauseating to me became sweetness and life." He marks that moment as conversion, when he "left the world" (the first half of his life). The leper was his stumbling-block, and he discovered in that encounter his sanctuary.

The invitation to the second journey—the key to spiritual transition and transformation—is almost always unexpected and unsought. If we seek spiritual heroism, the old ego is back in control, only in disguise. This is self-improvement on our terms, and not real change. Self-help projects of any type can only help us if they teach us to be mindful, to pay full attention to our lives and to life itself. Any attempt to engineer one's enlightenment is doomed to failure because it will be ego driven. So we must stumble and fall; failure and humiliation force us to look where we never would otherwise.

For much of the Western world today, life is conceived as all upward and onward, climbing the ladder of success by ourselves. It may work for a while, but it cannot serve us well in the long run because it is not true. In this scenario, life is a competition, an inherently win-lose game, and more and more people find themselves on the losing side, frustrated and disappointed. Even those who succeed "gain the world but lose their soul," as Jesus put it. They do their survival dance, but never get to the sacred dance, which by necessity includes others as well.

As noted earlier, the Gospels quote Jesus talking about "leaving" or even "hating" family in order to be his followers and thereby enter the Kingdom of God. To understand these imperatives, we need to revisit the biblical account of God asking Abraham to sacrifice his only son Isaac. As the existential philosopher Søren Kierkegaard made clear, there are three phases in the journey of faith: the aesthetic or sensual stage, the ethical stage, and the religious stage. The third stage is final because it follows the moral stage, when one embraces universal moral standards. As Kierkegaard notes, God is not asking Abraham to act immorally but rather to relate wholly to God through a life of faith, which transcends human morality, for to question God would be to place reason over faith, ego over trust. When Jesus calls for ultimate allegiance, he is undoing the fourth commandment of Moses, which tells us to "honor our father and mother." This commandment is necessary for the first half of life. But as we move into the second half of life, we are often at odds with our natural family, including the values and expectations of our dominant culture. The fact is that many people are kept from mature religion because of the pious, immature, or rigid expectations of their first-half-of-life family and upbringing. Even the family of Jesus thought he was "crazy" (Mark 3:21).

One of the major blocks against the second journey is our cultural mindset. What passes for morality or spirituality in the vast majority of people's lives is the way their peers think or live. Some might call this "conditioning" or even "imprinting." Without challenging inner work, most people never move beyond their cultural values and expectations. What Jesus is doing when he speaks of "hating" or leaving family and loved ones is using hyperbole to push us out of the comfort and security of the family nest. It takes quite a push, lots of self-doubt, and some degree of separation for individuals to find their own soul and destiny apart from what their family and friends want them to be and do. To move beyond inherited baggage, whether family-of-origin, local church, cultural, or patriotic stuff, is a path that few follow positively and with integrity. The pull is too great, and the loyal soldier fills us with appropriate guilt, shame, and self-doubt, which we easily but falsely interpret as the voice of God.

So Jesus pulls no punches. He tells us that we must leave home to find our real and larger home. The nuclear family often functions as the enemy of the global family and mature spiritual seeking. To some extent, one must also ask if "church family," meaning cherished dogmas and habitual priorities, is also a family that one has to eventually "hate" in this same way, with the same scandal involved as hating the natural family. In Matthew's Gospel, when Jesus declares that "those who want to save their life will lose it, and those who lose their life for my sake will find it" (16:25), the necessary suffering involved in "losing our life" has to do with what some call the "false self" or the false ego. The question becomes, how much false self are we willing to shed to find our True Self? Such necessary suffering will feel like dying, which Jesus and authentic spiritual teachers talk about honestly: "Very truly, I tell you, unless a grain of wheat falls into the earth and dies, it remains just a single grain; but if it dies, it bears much fruit" (John 12:24). As Rohr reminds us, if spiritual guides do not talk about dying, "they are not good spiritual guides!"[12]

Dying, however, is not the final word. For out of one's "death" new life emerges, a life of becoming fully and consciously who we already are, but

---

12. Ibid., 85.

it is a self that we largely do not know. All the dying and emptying is for the sake of a Great Outpouring, for God, like nature, abhors vacuums, and rushes to fill them. The task of midlife is to teach us and guide us on this discovery of our True Self.

Grant's Hypothesis

An important theory of human development was proposed by W. Harold Grant in *From Image to Likeness*, an approach to spirituality using the MBTI.[13] Building on the Great Commandment of Jesus for loving God with your heart (Feeling), soul (Intuition), mind (Thinking), and strength (Sensing), Grant suggests that these four functions, which develop uniquely and selectively in one's formative years, are employed in an integrated way after age fifty (midlife). Until age six, children live in an undifferentiated way typologically, but between six and twelve they begin to function in their dominant with its attitude, either Extraversion or Introversion. Age twelve, the time of rites of passage in world religions, is when the auxiliary function emerges as an attitude opposite from that of the earlier dominant, just in time for the abrupt changes of adolescence. Grant believes that between ages twenty to thirty-five, adults develop the tertiary function, and by midlife (ages thirty-five to fifty), the inferior function gains greater priority in one's life. At approximately age fifty the four cognitive functions come together to allow for a "second childhood" or a second blooming.

While Grant's six-stage hypothesis is useful as a reference point for discovery, it is limited in addressing the complexity of life, particularly at midlife. Terence Duniho suggests fourteen chronological cycles, while Robert and Carol Faucett see a much less ordered development that Grant's theory suggests. They believe that the dominant and auxiliary functions are developed by midlife, and after midlife the tertiary and inferior functions are developed, if all goes well. Even here the goals of wholeness and freedom are never "finally" reached. Carl Jung, concerned with differentiation and individuation through a lifetime of compensatory balancing, believed that the goal of spiritual growth is never exhausted. In his estimation, there is no final goal; indeed, stasis is a negative.

---

13. This segment is adapted from Richardson, *Four Spiritualities*, 26–27. For a discussion of type dynamics and type development, consult chapter 2 above.

Part II – The First Half of Life

Reinventing the Rites of Passage

In his Wheel of Life model, Bill Plotkin takes the four stages of human development—(a) childhood (rooted in innocence and wonder), (b) adolescence (rooted in mystery-probing adventure), (c) adulthood (rooted in cultural artistry), and (d) elderhood (rooted in care of the planet) and develops an eightfold pathway from the egocentrism to soulcentrism. Each stage contains a twofold developmental task: a nature task and a culture task. He characterizes egocentric societies as materialistic, anthropocentric, competition-based, class stratified, violence prone, and unsustainable, and soulcentric ones as imaginative, ecocentric, cooperation-based, just, compassionate, and sustainable.

He illustrates the intransigence of the first-half-of-living mindset by arguing that in modern industrial growth societies, the nature task is minimized as early as childhood, resulting in "an adolescence so out of sync with nature that most people never mature further."[14] Because industrial growth society engenders immature citizens unable to imagine a life beyond consumerism and soul-suppressing jobs, adults typically find themselves locked in pathological adolescence. Plotkin's eight-stage model shows the four stages of human development separated by five transitions. Each transitional event is an initiatory experience, whether or not formally marked by a rite of passage. The five transitions include (1) birth, (2) puberty, (3) soul initiation, (4) crowning[15] (where elderhood begins), and (5) death. The first transition, birth, is intended to initiate children into the wonders of innocence and nature; puberty enables young adolescents to acquire specific social and psychospiritual capacities that prepare them for adulthood; soul initiation represents a late adolescent shift in focus from social belonging and soul discovery to the active embodiment of soul in one's community; crowning represents the beginning of elderhood, at which time individuals turn from embodiment to a more expansive domain, the "soul of the more-than-human community"; and death represents the return of the individual to spirit. In Plotkin's conception, adolescence is when humans acquire the social and psychospiritual capacities that prepare them for "Soul Initiation," essential for the wellbeing of society and the planet because this experience represents "the radical transformation in life orientation in which humans

---

14. Plotkin, *Nature and the Human Soul*, 5.

15. At this transition, elders relinquish their conscious attachment to the embodiment of their individual souls—the definition of adulthood—and turn toward the tending of the soul of the larger-than human community, ibid., 59.

shift from a focus on social belonging and soul discovery to the active embodiment of soul in their community."[16] In adulthood, mature humans acquire and hone unique ways of serving their community through "soul-work." While these eight stages exist as possibilities for all humans, many, unfortunately, plateau in stage 3 (early adolescence), performing the task of that stage ("creating a secure and authentic social self") but unable to move successfully through stage 4 (late adolescence), with its twin tasks of "leaving home (the adolescent identity) and exploring the mysteries of darkness and the underworld."

Plotkin speaks of "three worlds" in which humans live, by which he means three realms of consciousness: upperworld, middleworld, and underworld. These correspond to spirit, ego, and soul respectively. Upperworld denotes transpersonal states of consciousness identified with spirit and characterized by unity, grace, bliss, transcendence, emptiness, light, enlightenment, the celestial realm, and pure consciousness. This state of consciousness is enhanced by activities such as meditation, prayer, contemplation, and yoga. Middleworld denotes everyday waking states of consciousness identified with ego and ego growth. Underworld signifies transpersonal states of consciousness identified with soul and characterized by depth, darkness, the subconscious, sacred wounding, dreams, shadow, death, and visions. This is the domain of soul encounters, where the conscious soul is deepened and matured. This state of consciousness is facilitated by practices Plotkin calls "soulcraft," including dreamwork, deep imagery journeys, wandering in nature, and communicating with nature.[17] The shared purpose of these three states of consciousness is: (1) transcending the conscious self (upperworld), (2) differentiating the conscious self (middleworld), and (3) deepening the conscious self (underworld).

For Stage 3, the phase of social individuation, Plotkin lists eight subtasks, which sound very much like Rohr's description of the first half of life:[18]

1. Exploring values and learning the skills of social authenticity
2. Emotional skills: emotional access, insight, action, and illumination

---

16. Plotkin, *Nature and the Human Soul*, 58.

17. For additional information on "soulcraft," consult Plotkin's book by that title.

18. The following lists of tasks and subtasks may be found in Plotkin's appendix: "Summary of Eco-Soulcentric Development," *Nature and the Human Soul*, 460–61. They are described more fully in the body of his text.

3. Art of conflict resolution (with both outer and inner conflicts)
4. Status-assigning skills
5. Skills in sex and sexual relationships
6. Sustenance skills
7. Studying human-nature reciprocity and ecological responsibility
8. Welcoming home the Loyal Soldier.

For Stage 4 (late adolescence), two tasks are given: (a) leaving home (relinquishing our adolescent identity) and (b) exploring the mysteries of nature and psyche.

Task 1 (leaving home) involves the following subtasks:

A. Honing the skills of physical, psychological, and social self-reliance

B. Relinquishing attachment to our adolescent identity

   1. Addressing developmental deficits from earlier stages
   2. Giving up addictions
   3. Exploring the sacred wound
   4. Learning to choose authenticity over social acceptance
   5. Making peace with the past
   6. Learning the art of disidentification through the practice of meditation

Task 2 (exploring the mysteries of nature and psyche) involves the following subtasks:

A. Acquiring and developing a set of soulcraft skills such as dreamwork, nature dialogues, deep imagery, trance drumming and dancing, sensitivity to signs and omens, soul poetry, symbolic artwork, and fasting

B. Cultivating a soulful relationship to life through practices and disciplines such as:

   1. The art of solitude
   2. Discovering nature as a mirror of the soul
   3. Wandering in nature
   4. Living the questions of soul
   5. Confronting our own death

The Middle Passage (The Work of Midlife)

6. The art of shadow work
7. The art of romance
8. Mindfulness practice
9. Service work
10. Advanced Loyal Soldier work
11. Developing the four dimensions of the Self
12. Praising the world
13. Developing a personal relationship with spirit
14. The art of being lost
15. Befriending the dark
16. Withdrawing projections

For our purposes, Plotkin's approach to spirituality is a model for the entirety of life, an idealized method that is more helpful to those mentoring children, adolescents, and young adults than for those in their later years who are cultivating second-half-of-life attitudes and behavior. In our case, what is most helpful about Plotkin's Wheel is his version of what we are calling the Midlife Passage and the Second Half of Life, which he frames in ecocentric and soulcentric terminology. Also beneficial is his understanding of the centrality of "Soul Initiation," without which one cannot pass into mature adulthood and beyond.

According to Plotkin, adolescence holds the key to becoming fully human, the potential to genuine adulthood. Adulthood is not biological, evolutionary, or based on chronological age, but is entered by an initiation process that requires (1) letting go of the familiar and comfortable and (2) submitting to a journey of descent into the mysteries of nature and the human soul. Older people, looking more deeply at their lives and spiritual development and grieved because they know that this is where they needed to go as adolescents but didn't, may qyestion whether it is too late.

Plotkin answers this question by (a) defining what constitutes passage to a stage of life (not chronological age or social status but by the progress made with the developmental tasks encountered at each stage), (b) indicating what progress means (every stage is fulfilling for a person in that stage; paradoxically, people must love the stage they are in in order to eventually leave it), (c) identifying the emotional suffering of transitioning from one stage to another (every transition is painful, involves loss, and entails a crisis for the conscious self), and (d) by emphasizing the expansiveness of the process (each successive stage brings new and greater opportunities for fulfillment and for growing more fully human). Progress can only be made one stage at a time, and only when one is fully ready will the next phase present itself to the initiate. One cannot skip a stage or the requisite initiations with the hope of returning later to finish their task, for there are no free passes in human or spiritual development.

While I find Plotkin's approach to human development intriguing, my intent in *Dark Splendor* is not to create a method, rulebook, or cookie-cutter model for others to replicate. Rather my intent is to provide a template which, like a mirror, can shed light on your place along the journey, illumine the dynamics of your inner life, enlarge your vision, and address you spiritual needs. Guidelines can be helpful, models can be beneficial, but when they become inflexible, they can turn into a methodology, a cult, or even another religion.

Can we revisit our past? Surely we can. We might not be able to change the past, but we can certainly change our trajectory in the present and for the future. We might need to find new tools for our spiritual toolkit or sharpen tools we received along the way, but we should never live with an unhealable past or with an intractable present. The future opens wide to those in midlife and beyond. When the outer and the inner journeys align, we are ready for "soul-making," a journey that takes time, effort, skill, knowledge, intuition, and courage. What is needed is to follow our heart—to follow our "bliss," as Joseph Campbell described it.

Spirituality and Theological Unlearning

If spirituality is more about unlearning than about learning, the first theological dogma one needs to unlearn is the doctrine of heaven and hell. We have learned that heaven is where good people—the "saved," namely God's beloved—spend an eternity with God, and that hell is where bad people—often non-Christians and even Christians "unsaved" according to in-group definitions—spend an eternity without God. It is far better to take these terms, as Jesus does in John's Gospel, as references to present experiences. The false self makes religion into an "evacuation plan for the next world," as Brian McLaren puts it, but the True Self knows that heaven is now and that its loss is hell now. In that respect it might be said that religion is for those afraid to go to hell, while spirituality is for those who have been there.

A person who has found his or her True Self has learned how to live in the big picture, as a part of deep time and all of history. This change of frame and venue is called living in the Kingdom of God by Jesus, and it necessitates that we let go of our own smaller kingdoms, what Earl Jabay calls "the kingdom of self," which people in the first half of life do not want to do. Life in the Kingdom of God is both practicing for heaven and living in heaven. When we do not know our True Self, we push all enlightenment into a possible future reward and punishment system, within which hardly anyone wins. When we live in God's Kingdom, we envision a more hopeful eternity. Ken Wilber described the later stages of life well when he said that "the classic spiritual journey always begins elitist and ends egalitarian."[19]

Heaven is the state of union both here and later. As now, so will it be then. No one is in heaven unless he or she wants to be, and all are in heaven when they live interdependently. That is biblical truth. People are in heaven when they "abide in Christ," living in love with one another, making room for fellowship with the divine, and thinking and living inclusively. The larger and more inclusive one's house is, the bigger one's heaven. Perhaps this is what Jesus meant by there being "many rooms in my Father's house" (John 14:2). If you go to heaven alone, wrapped in your private worthiness and narrow selectivity, it is by definition *not* heaven. The more you exclude, the more hellish and lonely your existence always is. How could anyone enjoy heaven knowing their loved ones were not there, or were being tortured for all eternity? If you accept a punitive notion of God, who eternally punishes and tortures those who do not love him, then you have an absurd universe where most people on earth end up being more loving than God. Why would Jesus' love be unconditional while he was in this world, and suddenly become totally conditional after his death? How could Jesus ask us to bless, forgive, and heal our enemies, which he clearly does (Matt. 5:43–48), unless God is doing it first and always? Be assured, no one is in hell unless that individual chooses final aloneness and separation.

The second theological dogma one needs to unlearn is the doctrine of sin and salvation. John 3:16, the most quoted verse in the New Testament, sums up the message of Jesus by reiterating the salvific dimension of Jesus' death, but moves the argument forward with its reference to God's love. This passage indicates that God's love is directed toward "the world," a term

---

19. Cited by Rohr, *Falling Upward*, 103.

generally associated with that part of humanity that is at odds with Jesus and God. In John 3:16–18, called the "Gospel in miniature," we learn that Jesus' purpose in coming is not for the purpose of passing judgment, but rather for the purpose of turning people to God. The context makes clear that Jesus is God's gift of love to everyone, though only believers accept the gift.

The reason that Jesus does not come to pass judgment is because people judge themselves by their response to Jesus. This interpretation is seen in the story of the healing of the blind man in John 9, in crucial ways an exposition of 3:16–21. This story is not simply about the restoration of natural sight. Rather, the author uses this healing story to portray the process of spiritual decision-making. Light and darkness are no longer merely concepts, but are embodied by the characters portrayed in the story. In the blind man's journey from physical blindness to spiritual sight, readers are able to watch as someone comes to the light and is given new life. In the Jewish authorities' passage from physical sight to spiritual blindness, readers are able to watch as the religious authorities close themselves to the light and place themselves under judgment. The dramatic structure of this passage intensifies the profound theological irony: the authorities, who position themselves as judges of others, finally bring themselves under judgment as sinners.

The presentation of sin in John 9 is pivotal to the understanding of sin in John, where the self-righteousness of the Pharisees becomes the basis for their judgment as sinners: "If you were blind, you would not have sin. But now that you say, 'We see,' your sin remains" (John 9:41). In its deepest and most illuminating sense, sin in the Bible is defined not by what one does or does not do, but almost exclusively by one's relationship to God. In the New Testament, believers are asked to recognize the transformative power of the love of God and to shape their lives accordingly. To reject Jesus is to reject the love of God in Jesus and so to pass from the possibility of salvation to judgment. The blind man's words in John 9:25 offer eloquent testimony to the transforming power of God's grace in the hymn "Amazing Grace": "I once was blind, but now I see."

The third and final theological dogma one needs to unlearn concerns the person of Jesus Christ, the doctrine known as Christology.[20] For all practical purposes, the dualist mind is not able to accept the orthodox teaching that Jesus is both fully human and fully divine simultaneously. Rationalist thinking needs to split and divide, with the result that it understands

---

20. The segment on Christology has been adapted from Rohr, *Naked Now*, 67–79.

The Middle Passage (The Work of Midlife)

Jesus as *only* divine and understands humans as *only* human, despite all scriptural and mystical affirmation to the contrary. The doctrine of the Incarnation was designed to overcome this divide, but the practical results for individual Christians, as for Christianity, have been disastrous.

The application of the "I Am" title to Jesus, central to the Fourth Gospel, so thrilled early Christians that they forgot the continued need to balance this discovery with Jesus' even more strongly proclaimed humanity. In the Synoptic Gospels, virtually Jesus' only form of self-reference was "son of man," meaning "son of the human one." This is the same phrase used repeatedly by the prophet Ezekiel, who uses it as reference to his mortality and humanity. Early Christian theologians knew this, but they went to an obscure passage in Daniel 7:14 for background, a difficult apocalyptic text with symbolic meaning. When Jesus spoke of himself as "son of man," he most certainly was emphasizing his humanity.

Our Christology impacts our anthropology, meaning that our view of Jesus impacts how we view ourselves. Since Christians mostly think of Jesus as having only a divine nature (for that is how they explain Jesus' ability to perform miracles), they miss a major point he made about himself. Because dualist minds are unable to balance humanity and divinity in Jesus, they are unable to put it together concerning themselves. This is a powerful point, with major implications for Christian thinking and living. If our conception is limited to either one view or another, eliminating the possibility that it can be both, the result is that we think of ourselves as mere humans trying desperately to become "spiritual," and of Jesus as a divine being trying to look human. The Christian truth is quite different: we are already spiritual (we bear God's divine image), and our task is to become more fully human. Jesus came to model the full integration for us and, in effect, "told us that divinity looked just like him—while he looked ordinarily human to everybody!"[21]

Such mystery is the ultimate paradox, and each Christian and every human struggles with it anew, both in themselves and in Jesus. Over time Christians were unable to hold this mystery of Jesus intact, with the result that they were unable to see, honor, and reconcile the mystery inside themselves and in others. Nondualist thinking allows us to affirm "the infinite mystery of Jesus and the infinite mystery that we are to ourselves. They are finally the same mystery."[22] What Augustine said about God, "If you

---

21. Ibid., 69.
22. Ibid., 70.

understand, then it is not God," we can say about Jesus and about ourselves: "If we understand the Mystery, then it is not so."

In a remarkable statement, addressed both to Pharisees and to his disciples—and therefore to outsiders and insiders simultaneously—Jesus states that the Kingdom (the Ultimate Reality) is "not here and not there" but rather "within you" (Luke 17:21). What Jesus is saying, in effect, is that God's actions and presence cannot be limited to sacred times or sacred places, as we understand them, "for the ultimate sacred reality is within you!"

Jesus humbles much of organized religion's capacity to control the God-human relationship because Jesus is saying that God is always beyond any attempt to be controlled. Jesus is "protecting the utter freedom of God to be *where* God wants and *when* God wants and *who* God wants."[23] Good theology, like Luke's, always protects God's freedom.

We must never forget that God loves us because God is good, not because we are good. That changes everything.

---

23. Ibid., 77.

Part III – The Second Half of Life

CHAPTER 6

A Second Simplicity

> Now is the time, if ever it is to happen, for you to answer
> the summons of the soul, to live the second, larger life.
> —JAMES HOLLIS

THE SECOND-HALF-OF-LIFE JOURNEY HAS been likened to the postcritical phase of life or a second simplicity. Paul Ricoeur speaks of it as a second naiveté or a second childhood. Whatever we call it, I believe this condition is the very goal of mature adulthood and mature religion. First naiveté is the earnest and dangerous innocence we sometimes admire in young zealots, but it is also the reason we should not elect them or follow them as leaders. It is probably necessary to be impetuous when we are young, taking risks and eliminating most doubt. In the long run such approaches to life are not wise. Mature wisdom is content to live with mystery, doubt, and "unknowing," and in such living ironically resolves that very mystery to some degree. It takes a great deal of learning to finally "learn ignorance," as so many religious sages discovered. As T. S. Eliot puts it in the *Four Quartets*: "We had the experience but missed the meaning." This means, at least in part, that people in the second half of life need not expect to have the same experiences as others; rather, simple meaning now suffices.

This new coherence, a unified field that embraces paradox, is precisely what gradually characterizes a second-half-of-life person. It feels like a return to simplicity after having learned from all the complexity. Finally one understands that "everything belongs," even the sad, absurd, and futile parts. In the second half of life we can devote ourselves to integrating even the painful parts of our life into the now unified field, including people who are different or marginalized. If you can forgive yourself for being imperfect and falling, you can now do it for just about everybody else.

Some people seem to have missed out on the joy and clarity of the first simplicity, perhaps avoided the interim complexity, and finally lost the great freedom and magnanimity of the second simplicity as well. We need to hold together all of the stages of life, and for some reason it all becomes quite "simple" as we approach our later years.

As previously noted, the transformation that brings us to the second half of life is often more about unlearning than learning. Perhaps it is simply a more profound learning. Life is more spacious now, the boundaries of the container having been enlarged by transformative experiences and relationships. For many people, the second half of life is characterized by seven transformational qualities:[1]

1. Less fear and therefore less hostility. Because one has less need to eliminate the negative or fearful from one's life, there is less need to punish other people. Superiority complexes have been shown to be useless, ego based, counterproductive, and often entirely wrong.

2. Less combative. By the second half of life one has learned that most frontal attacks simply add to the amount of evil within. Along with an inflated self-image, they incite retaliation from those one has attacked.

3. Less need of attention. When "elders" speak, they need few words to make their point. Second simplicity has its own kind of brightness and clarity, but much of it is expressed nonverbally, and only when really needed. In the first half of life, one is defined through differentiation; now one looks for commonality. One does not need to dwell on the differences between people or exaggerate the problems. Creating dramas has become boring.

4. Less assertive. In the second half of life it is good just to be a part of the general dance. We do not have to stand out or be better than others; life is more participatory than assertive, and there is no need for strong or further self-definition.

5. Less self-concerned. At this stage we no longer have to prove that we are the best, that our ethnicity is superior, our religion the only one accepted by God, or that our role and place in society deserve special treatment.

---

1. The following points are adapted from Rohr, *Falling Upward*, 118–125.

6. Less dogmatic. People in the second half of life are less condemning. They no longer see God as small, punitive, or tribal. They once defended signposts; now they have arrived where the signs pointed. One's growing sense of spaciousness is no longer found mostly "out there" but especially "in here." The inner and the outer have become one. In the second journey, we have less final opinions about things and people as we allow them to delight or sadden us. We no longer need to change or adjust other people in order to be happy ourselves. Ironically, we are more than ever before in a position to change others—but we do not need to—and that makes all the difference. Now we aid and influence others simply by being who we are.

7. Less possessive. At this stage we are no longer preoccupied with accumulating additional goods and services; rather, our desire and effort should be to pay back to the world some of what we have received. Our concern is not so much to have what you love but to love what you have—here and now. This is such a monumental change from the first half of life that it is almost the litmus test of whether one is in the second half of life at all.

This is the falling upward of which Rohr speaks. "Such inner brightness," he concludes, "ends up being a much better and longer-lasting alternative to evil than any war, anger, violence, or ideology could ever be. All you have to do is meet one such shining person and you know that he or she is surely the goal of humanity and the delight of God."[2]

Such transformation requires six steps: (1) forgiveness (repudiating retaliation or "getting even"); (2) prayer (learning to listen in silence); (3) changing one's attitude ("unlearning"); (4) quiet persuasion (becoming an elder statesman); (5) becoming an agent of change (which starts with actively working for peace); and (6) influencing events (indirectly rather than directly, by modeling the transformative qualities of the second simplicity).

If unlearning is a way to deeper spirituality, the following pathways represent "paradigm shifts," attitudinal transformations, in the journey from the first to the second half of life:

- Impatience to greater patience;
- Critical to more accepting;
- Pessimism to optimism;

2. Ibid., 125.

Part III – The Second Half of Life

- Stoical to joyful;
- Independent to dependent;
- Aloof to affectionate;
- Self-centered to other-oriented
- Frugal to generous.

Again, these observations do not represent precepts to be followed or new commandments to be obeyed. The second half of life is not about precepts or commandments, for there is only one guideline for the second half of life: to love the Lord your God with your entire mind, heart, soul, and strength, and your neighbor as yourself. The rest is commentary.

The second half of life is certainly paradoxical. The normal progression in the United States and throughout most of the Western world is that one's world enlarges as one grows older. However, in the second half of life, as we have been describing it, one's circle of close friends and confidants normally diminishes, yet becomes more intimate and vital. One is no longer surprised or angered when most people—and even institutions—are doing first-half-of-life tasks.

Our question now becomes, "how can we honor the legitimate needs of the first half of life, while creating space, vision, time, and grace for the second?" For Rohr, "The holding of this tension is the very shape of wisdom."[3] While becoming impatient with institutions, including the church, second-journey believers should maintain contact with institutions such as government and the church, not so much for one's own sake, but for the sake of the institution. All institutions need second-half-of-life people in their ranks; just a few in each organization may be enough to keep them from total self-interest. However, one should not expect or demand from groups what they usually cannot give: they must and will be concerned with identity, boundaries, self-maintenance, self-perpetuation, and self-congratulation. This is their nature and purpose. In your second half of life, you can actually bless others in what they feel they must do, challenging them if you must, but you can no longer join them in the first half of life. You can belong to such institutions for all the good that they do, but you will not fully engage with them. This will keep you and others from unnecessary frustration, anger, and futility.

---

3. Ibid., 138.

A Second Simplicity

If one can say that the first half of life defines itself by "no" and the second half of life by "yes," there will be a certain and real loneliness if you are saying "yes" while your old friends, groups, and even churches are saying "no." However—and here is the silver lining—to those who are experiencing rejection and loss, the second half of life promises a new ability to be alone—and to be happy alone. One of the great surprises at this point is the discovery that "the cure for your loneliness is actually solitude!"[4] First, there is the realization that one is not alone, that one is part of the whole community, the whole of time, space, nature, and supernature. Next, silence, music, and poetry become our more natural voice and our more beautiful ear at this stage. Much of life starts becoming highly symbolic and interconnected. Silence, we eventually discover, becomes the only lexicon spacious enough to include all things and to keep us from sliding back into dualistic judgments and divisive words. As a result, our political, social, and economic views become more compassionate and inclusive. A kind of "double belonging" characterizes people at this stage. No one group meets all of their needs, desires, and visions. One becomes more attracted to progressive and expansive moments within the church and society. What this illustrates, of course, is the capacity for "nondualistic" thinking or "both-and" thinking.

Dualistic thinking, of course, is a pattern of knowing most things by comparison, judging or labeling something as good and the other as less good or even bad. Ultimately most things become categorized according to moral, theological, or preferential polarities. The normal sequencing of the dualist mind, dubbed the seven C's of delusion, consist of the following judgmental activity: it compares, competes, conflicts, conspires, condemns, cancels out contrary evidence, and then it crucifies.

Nondualistic or contemplative thinking emerges during the second half of life. One's frame grows larger as one embraces the Big Picture in which "one God creates all and loves all, Dodgers and Yankees, blacks and whites, Palestinians and Jews, Americans and Afghanis."[5] This perspective is almost certainly the benchmark of our growth into the second half of life. One no longer needs to divide people and situations into totally right or totally wrong, with me or against me. In the second half of life, all that you avoided for the sake of a manufactured ego ideal starts coming back as a true friend and teacher. Doers become thinkers, feelers become doers, thinkers become feelers, extroverts become introverts, visionaries become practical, and prac-

4. Ibid., 143.
5. Ibid., 148.

tical ones long for vision. We all gravitate toward the very places we avoided for the last forty years, and our friends are amazed. Now we begin to understand why Jesus is always welcoming the outsider, the foreigner, the sinner, the wounded one. He was a second-half-of-life man who had the unenviable task of trying to teach and be understood by a largely first-half-of-life culture and church. Jesus may well have been the first nondualistic religious thinker in the West (there were philosophers like Heraclitus, but his teachings were quickly filtered through Greek dualistic logic).

Unless you let the truth of life teach you on its own terms, unless you develop some concrete practice for recognizing and overcoming your dualistic mind, you will remain in the first half of life forever, as most of humanity has up to now. In the first half of life, you cannot work with the imperfect, nor can you accept the tragic sense of life, which finally means that you cannot love anything or anyone at any depth. Nothing is going to change in history as long as most people remain dualistic, either-or thinkers.

Whole people see and create wholeness wherever they go; split people see and create fragmentation in everything and everybody. The unified field, represented by the second-half-of-life existence, is the only and lasting meaning of "up." We are all familiar with Helen Keller, who was blind, deaf, and mute. She seems to have leaped into the second half of life in the chronological first half of her life, once she discovered her depths. She lived most of her life happy and fulfilled, convinced that life was about service to others and not about protecting and lamenting her severe physical limitations.

That seems to be the great difference between transformed and nontransformed people. Transformed people live to serve, not to be served. It is a perspective good parents exemplify. Many of the happiest, most generous and focused people are young mothers. Whole people see and create wholeness wherever they go.

I once asked my wife Susan, a second-half person, to identify her tasks for the second journey. She responded succinctly yet profoundly:

1. Identifying and affirming one's core self
2. Deepening friendships
3. Accepting one's death
4. Redefining one's belief system.

"What about God," I asked? "Where is God in this process?"

"God is in all of these," she replied, agreeing with Paula D'Arcy that "God comes to you disguised as your life."

CHAPTER 7

Regaining Soul

For all the changes that have occurred over the last four centuries, perhaps our greatest loss is the diminution of dialogue about that mystery toward which the word *soul* is meant to point.

—JAMES HOLLIS

FOR SEVERAL HUNDRED YEARS modern society has convinced people in the West that progress, human reason, and higher technology would suffice human need and resolve the human dilemma. Clearly they have not. Progress has too often been achieved at a high cost, at the expense of the earth and the health of the human spirit. More analysis does not necessarily mean more wisdom, and having more options is not necessarily freedom. The accumulation of things is not likely to bring more happiness, and time saved is rarely used for contemplation. According to psychotherapist Thomas Moore, the great malady of modernity is "loss of soul." Modern people have not only lost their soul, they have lost wisdom about the soul, even interest in it. But when soul is neglected or ignored, it doesn't simply go away; "it appears symptomatically in obsessions, addictions, violence, and loss of meaning."[1]

It is difficult to define precisely what "soul" is. In order to better understand the concept, I prefer to begin with an ontological model described by Huston Smith as "Levels of Selfhood."[2] According to Smith, the human self consists of four levels, configured concentrically as (1) body, (2) mind, (3) soul, and (4) spirit. Whereas Smith places the body in the innermost circle, as the most accessible aspect, with the other levels expanding con-

---

1. Moore, *Care of the Soul*, xi.
2. Smith, *Forgotten Truth*, 60–95.

centrically outward to the spirit, humanity's most expansive element, I think of the body as the outermost level, the container for the inner levels of selfhood. Next is the mind, the seat of consciousness, conceived as distinct from the brain, which is a part of the body. This distinction is based on the perspective of neurophysiologists such as Wilder Penfield, who argue for the uniqueness of the mind, which "seems to act independently of the brain in the same sense that a programmer acts independently of his computer."[3] According to Smith, there is no convincing materialistic explanation of mind, for mind cannot be measured quantitatively. Furthermore, mind plays by different rules, conforming to laws that differ in kind from those that matter exemplifies.

The third level of selfhood is the soul (called by ancients *psyche, anima, atman, nephesh,* or *nafs*), the final locus of our individuality, its source and yet superior. The soul is closer to our essence than is the mind, with which we usually identify; its tropism is toward being and its increase.[4] While the soul is finite, it is the only possible bridge to Spirit, the fourth level of selfhood. If soul is the element in humans that relates to God, Spirit is the element that is identical with God, not with God's personal mode but with God's mode that is infinite. Mystics and theologians speak of identity at this level because "on this final stratum the subject-object dichotomy is transcended."[5] While Spirit is infinite, humans remain finite because they are not Spirit only. Our specifically human overlay—body, mind, and soul—veils the Spirit within us.

The key point in Smith's model is the realization that as far as selfhood is concerned, one cannot maintain harmony, equilibrium, and flow by jumping across levels. Each level builds consecutively and concentrically on the preceding. In other words, the bridge to consciousness is the body. To understand the mind, one must be fully grounded in one's physicality. The link to soul is mind, and the link to Spirit is soul. Each level must be explored deeply and authentically before it can serve as conduit to the next. To acquire meaning and understanding, one cannot jump from body to soul or from mind to Spirit. For Smith, the final link, the door that leads from soul to spirit, is love: love of "Being-as-a whole or of the God who is its Lord. For Spirit to permeate the self's entirety, the components of the

---

3. Ibid., 64.
4. Ibid., 76.
5. Ibid., 87.

self must be aligned: body in temperance, mind in understanding, and soul in love."[6]

We live in a time of deep division, in which mind is at odds with body and spirituality with matter. We need a way out of the dualistic attitudes that permeate our thinking, permeable boundaries between polarities such as good and evil, God and Satan, light and darkness, spirit and flesh, eternal life and eternal death, belief and disbelief, truth and falsehood, heaven and hell, heaven and earth. Dualism claims independent reality for each polarity, whereas the truth is that the negative item in the pair derives somehow from its opposite. As cold is the absence of heat, so evil is the absence of good, and so forth. As the book of Revelation makes clear, soft boundaries exist between spatial and temporal planes and even between good and evil. Evil contrasts from good, but evil is not of a fundamentally different order from good. Even God and Satan, the epitome of good and evil respectively, are not separated by hard, impervious boundaries, for in the Bible the "demonic" plane derives from the heavenly, divine plane. While boundaries do exist between heaven and earth, future and present, deity and humanity, and good and evil, there is dynamism to boundaries. Boundaries do not fix limits beyond which it is impossible to pass. Rather they locate the place where transformations occur, allowing a flow across planes, eras, social categories, and moral values.

In the Bible, "heaven" is the starting point for all revelation. We should not, however, restrict "heaven" to the spiritual dimension of reality, for it represents more than that. In the book of Revelation, what John sees in heaven is not simply divine perspective. Heaven represents what is right and good and proper. When Jesus tells his followers to pray, "Your kingdom come . . . on earth as it is in heaven" (Matt. 6:10), he understands "heaven" not as a future destination for humans but as God's dimension of everyday reality. Heaven is in charge; heaven takes the lead; heaven represents what ought to be happening on earth.

What we need to take us out of dualistic attitudes is something nondualistic, not mind over body but a third possibility, and that third is soul. Soul, like poetry, seeks to hold together what seems to belong apart. The mind has a tendency to go off on its own so that at times it seems to have little relevance to the physical world. At the same time, the materialistic life can so absorb the senses that we forget about spirituality. What we need is something that holds together mind and body, ideas and life, spirituality

6. Ibid., 92.

and the world, spirit and intellect, and that is the role of soul. Like poetry, soul provides insight, wisdom, vision, language, and music.

According to Moore, "soul" is not a thing but "a quality or dimension of experiencing life and ourselves. It has to do with depth, value, relatedness, heart, and personal substance."[7] Carl Jung equated the unconscious with the soul, and so when we try to live fully consciously in an intellectually predictable world, protected from all mysteries and comfortable with conformity, we lose our everyday opportunities for the soulful life. Whereas the intellect wants to know, the soul likes to be surprised; the intellect wants external enlightenment, the soul seeks inward contemplation. When our spirituality isn't sufficiently profound, it often takes bizarre forms. When spirituality loses soul, it takes on fundamentalism, a defense against the richness of imagination.

There are many different kinds of spirituality. The kind with which we are most familiar is the spirituality of transcendence, "the lofty quest for the highest vision, universal moral principles, and liberation from many limitations of human life."[8] Other spiritualities are naturalistic (such as the spirituality of a place), or humanistic (whereby one focuses on family and honored traditions), or secular (where the focus is on widely varied areas of life such as beauty, enjoyment, sensuality, athletic competition, career, volunteerism, and social justice). If we can get past various fundamentalist attitudes about the spiritual life, such as attachment to a simplistic code of morality, fixed interpretation of stories, and communities where individual thinking is not valued, then many different ways of being spiritual emerge. "We may discover that there are ways to be spiritual that do not counter the soul's needs for body, individuality, imagination, and exploration. Eventually we might find that all emotions, all human activities, and all spheres of life have deep roots in the mysteries of the soul, and therefore are holy."[9]

By now we are aware that the soul is not the ego. It is the infinite depth of a person, comprising all the many mysterious aspects that go together to make up our identity. Soul is more interested in particulars than in generalities. That is true of personal identity as well. Identifying with a group or a syndrome or a diagnosis is giving in to an abstraction. Soul provides a strong sense of individuality—personal destiny, special influences and background, and unique stories. Therefore, care of the soul begins in the

---

7. Moore, *Care of the Soul*, 5.
8. Ibid., 140.
9. Ibid., 242.

simple telling of one's story. Soul is always in process, hence it is difficult to pin down with definition or a fixed meaning. When spirituality loses contact with soul, it can become rigid, simplistic, moralistic, and authoritarian—qualities that betray a loss of soul.

It should be clear that we are not using the word "soul" as popularly conceived, whether as an object of religious belief or as something to do with immortality. Soul is not about transcendence. Soul-work seeks more intimacy between consciousness and the body, between our body and the world's body, and between us and our fellow human beings. It basks in the imagination its methods bring.

It has been said that the soul is that which makes us human. Depth psychology turns that idea around and notes that it is when we are most human that we have greatest access to soul. The ultimate care for soul comes not from logic, psychotherapy, or religious diligence, but from taking an interest in it, giving it priority, which is a way of loving it.

Spirituality and soulfulness, which make up the fundamental pulse of life, have a fundamental attraction to one another. In our spirituality, we reach for consciousness, awareness, and the highest values; in our soulfulness, we endure the most pleasurable and the most exhausting of human experiences and emotions. Throughout life, if we nurture them and give them conscious priority, their attraction leads to a courtship, and at key moments, they wed. The ultimate marriage of spirit and soul is the wedding of heaven and earth, our highest ideals and ambitions united with our lowliest symptoms and complaints.

We live in a time of materialism and consumerism, of lost values and a shift in ethical standards. We find ourselves tempted to call for a return to old values and ways. Many feel that the best way forward is to turn to the past, when it seems we were more religious as a people and that traditional values had more influence throughout society. But the key to lost spirituality and numbing materialism is neither in nostalgic wishing for a return to former conditions nor in intensifying our quest for spirituality. The key, rather, is to reimagine spirituality, for spirituality and materialism can be trapped in a polarizing split: the more compulsively materialist we are, the more neurotic our spirituality will be, and vice versa. The cure for such a split is to establish soul in the middle, between spirit and body, as a way to prevent the two from becoming extreme caricatures of one another. The cure for materialism then is to find concrete ways of getting soul back into our spiritual practices, our intellectual life, and our emotional and physical engagements with the world.

Soul knows the relativity of its claim on truth. Soul is always facing a mirror, watching itself discover its developing truth, knowing that subjectivity and imagination are always in play. Truth is not really a soul word; soul is after insight more than truth. Truth is a stopping point; insight invites further exploration. Intellect tends to enshrine its truth, while soul hopes that insights will keep coming until some degree of wisdom is achieved. "Wisdom is the marriage of intellect's longing for truth and soul's acceptance of the labyrinthine nature of the human condition."[10] As Moore reminds us, "we are not going to have a soulful spirituality until we begin to think in the ways of soul. If we bring only the intellect's modes of thought to our search for a path or to spiritual practices, then from the very beginning we will be without soul. . . . Therefore a soul-oriented spirituality begins in a reevaluation of the qualities of soul: subtlety, complexity, ripening, worldliness, incompleteness, ambiguity, wonder."[11]

Faith, on the other hand, is a gift of spirit that allows the soul to remain attached to its own unfolding. When faith is soulful, it is always planted in the soil of wonder and questioning. It isn't a defensive and anxious holding on to certain objects of belief, because doubt can be brought into a faith that is fully mature. In soul faith there are always at least two figures—the "believer" and the "disbeliever." Questioning, drifting temporarily from commitments, change in one's understanding of faith—to the intellect these may appear to be weaknesses, but to the soul they are necessary and creative aspects that actually strengthen faith by ridding it of its perfectionism. Both belief and doubt play constructive roles in a well-rounded faith. The third part of the triangle is life in the flesh lived with deep trust.

The goal of the soul path is not to overcome life's struggles and anxieties, but to know life first hand, to exist fully in context. While spiritual practice is sometimes described as walking in the footsteps of another, the soul's odyssey is better described as walking a path (perhaps it is better to speak of a labyrinth, a meandering, or a wandering) no one has ever gone before.

Spiritually speaking, humans are always in union with God. But it is hard for people to believe or experience this when they have no positive sense of identity, little courage, no strong boundaries to contain sacred mystery, and little inner religious experience at any depth. Thus the first journey

10. Ibid., 246–47.
11. Ibid., 247.

is necessarily about externals, formulas, dogmas, correct rituals, scriptural literalism, prescriptive morality, and decorum, all of which largely substitute for actual spirituality. Yet they are all necessary to create the container. Early-stage religion is largely preparing us for the inner experience of God, which consoles our True Self only after it has devastated our false self. It is as if the first journey creates a feeding trough, later transformed into a proper stable into which the Christ is born. Unfortunately, most people get so preoccupied with their trough, and whether it is better than some else's trough, and whether their trough is the only "holy, catholic, and apostolic" trough, that they never get to the birth of God in their soul.[12]

Many church people, facing transformative social and personal issues, including marital failure, spiritual inadequacy, racism, gender equality, or any radical reading of the gospel, are often bored or limited by the typical Sunday church agenda. They are good people, but they keep on doing their own kind of survival dance, because no one has told them about their sacred dance. Our institutions and expectations, including our churches, are almost entirely configured to encourage, support, reward, and validate the tasks of the first half of life. Like many institutions, individuals in the church are more struggling to survive than to thrive, more just "getting by" or trying to get to the top than finding out what is really at the top or was already at the bottom. Thomas Merton, the Trappist monk, pointed out that many spend their whole life climbing the ladder of success, only to find when they get to the top that their ladder was leaning against the wrong wall.

---

12. Rohr, *Falling Upward*, 13–14.

CHAPTER 8

Soulcraft

> Older folks ought to be explorers
> Here and there does not matter
> We must be still and still moving
> Into another intensity
> For another union, a deeper communion.
>
> —T. S. ELIOT

Pathways to Soulfulness

THOUGH MANY HAVE TRIED, no one can chart another person's spiritual journey, just as no one can prescribe another person's moral values. Likewise, the ingredients of one's spiritual vision are established individually and personally and are applicable only to that individual.

The trajectory of one's second-half journey is best established by returning to the foundations of spirituality. Each person must select pathways that are attractive and effective. In my case, the following pathways stand out as particularly meaningful, together shaping the contours of my second-half-of-life spirituality: simplicity, stillness (silence), study, stamina, and service. The role of soul is to hold together what seems to belong apart.

The following model depicts how such pathways interrelate:

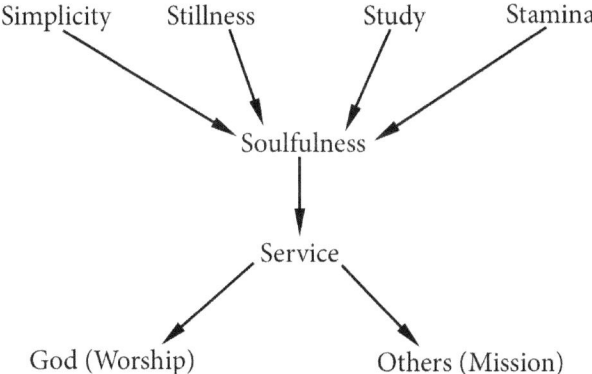

Simple and stark, these concepts are transformative when they are engaged together toward selfless and therapeutic ends. The harmony that is our goal involves the full effort of physical, emotional, and spiritual maturity, but what encourages this pursuit is the promise of integration on all levels of our being. At its deepest and most promising level, spirituality provides wholeness, bringing together body, mind, soul, and spirit.

By living such foundations we avoid the twin dangers of pietism and functionalism. The spiritual life is neither a matter of trans-worldly ascetical practices, leading to self-authenticating piety, nor of social activism, leading to functional, this-worldly reform while neglecting spiritual sustenance. If the first exaggeration breeds spiritual elitism, the second is subject to mood swings, from elation over projects accomplished to depression over projects abandoned or unfulfilled.

Reality is helplessness, aging, suffering, dying. It is vulnerability and lack of control. It is what we refuse to see because it is so near. Authentic spirituality calls us to face reality and to go through it to visions of redemption, rebirth, peace, and joy. All else passes, but the service we render to others is best fulfilled when we help keep the vision of hope from disappearing entirely.

The Human Body: Bane or Blessing?

One of the great tragedies of religious history occurred when the physical body was falsely accused for the sins of humanity. The idea that our most basic bodily functions, including our sensual pleasure and sexual passion, are unclean and unholy is not only a regrettable belief system, it is also profoundly ignorant. In her book *The Seeker's Guide*, Elizabeth Lesser affirms that "[d]eep spirituality is not an out-of-body experience; it's an in-body experience."[1] Body and mind are not separate; neither are body and emotions or body and soul. Humans are not spiritual beings trapped in a carnal existence. The self is like a diamond, each part a facet of the same essence. When we view our bodies as base and vulgar and our souls and spirits as pure and distinct, we affirm dualism, the bane of spirituality. If we recognize our bodies to be "materialized spirit," and therefore spiritually based, we are on our way to wholeness and truth. Care of the body, therefore, is the first and most important principle of religion. If we are to make spiritual progress, we must learn to love and care for our bodies. This is the starting premise of all healthy spirituality.

As we progress inward, following Huston Smith's model, we come to mind. The mind is not our thoughts, but rather a container for life's continual, creative impulses. If you examine your thoughts, you find that they are in constant flux, rolling across the landscape of your mind. Like the weather, sometimes our thoughts are sunny and bright, other times cloudy, and occasionally stormy. The mind by nature is intent on judging, controlling, and analyzing instead of seeing, tasting, and loving. The mind wants a job processing things, something it does well. But it cannot be fully present, doing the work of soul or spirit. The key to stopping the mind's game is quite simply peace, silence, and stillness. Our forbearers learned to control the mind and awaken its deepest potential through the practice of meditation. Meditation does not make things miraculously change, but it does create mindfulness, promoting awareness, acceptance, and integration.

Meditation is a matter of experience. It is a way to be fully present, to be genuinely who we are and need to be. Meditation is a way to look deeply at the nature of things, a way to discover the peace and wholeness we already possess. It does not aim to get rid of the bad or to create anything good. It is an attitude of openness. One does not practice meditation to become a great meditator, but to become skilled at the art of living. Some discipline is required, such as breath control, posture, time commitment, and a place free of distraction, all ways of stilling the mind in order that it might be renewed and reenergized.

The false ego will fight back, using defense mechanisms such as pain, restlessness, sleepiness, and self-judgment, but those who persevere will

---

1. Lesser, *Seeker's Guide*, 242.

move forward to soulfulness, which thrives on Simplicity and Silence and results in Service.

1. Simplicity Means Having Whatever You Want

The journey of spirituality begins with the realization that it is possible to live happily in the present moment. Imagine you are a child walking by a bakery. You see many delicious items inside and the aroma is enticing. Imagine the owner inviting you in and saying, "You can have whatever you want. The whole shop is for you." How would you react? And where would you begin?

When we come home to the present moment, filled with innumerable wonderful things and so many opportunities for happiness, we may feel like that child. How do we respond? And where do we begin? This is the opportunity we all face, and the key to success is simplicity. We can begin with mindfulness—mindful breathing, thinking, and action—and see whether we can handle the beauty and happiness that life offers. It is important that we cultivate our capacity for happiness, realizing that happiness is only available in the present.

When we are mindful of something, we naturally concentrate on it. If we hold a delicious ice cream cone, and concentrate on that cone, mindfulness enhances both the flavor and the experience. Our focus is not on the past, the future, or lost on other projects. The cone is the object of our concentration, and in that moment we are happy. When we are mindful of something, we naturally concentrate on it; when we are mindful and concentrated, insight arises. Insight makes us happy, because insight is liberating. If we are fearful, we cannot be joyful or content. If we worry, we can't be peaceful or happy. But when we have insight, fear and worry are removed and true happiness is possible.

Looking superficially, we might be annoyed when it rains or snows. But when we understand deeply, we perceive that rain and snow are wonderful, renewing and refreshing the earth year round. Looking deeply—mindfully, simply—enables us to enjoy all things, and life becomes enjoyable. Buddhists have a word for this condition, *samtusta*, which means that we have enough in our lives to make us happy, that what we have is sufficient.[2] *Samtusta* can also be translated as "the awareness that one is satisfied with little."

---

2. The discussion on *samtusta* in this segment is adapted from Hanh, *Good Citizens*, 58–60.

Part III – The Second Half of Life

When one is aware of the conditions of happiness already present in one's life, one usually finds that they are more than enough for present happiness.

We all know people without a big house or a new car who are content with what they have. We also know people who have plenty of money, power, and success who are deeply unhappy. We can't receive wellbeing and happiness from others. Each of us must walk the path for ourselves, practicing living happily in the present. *Samtusta*—non-craving—may be difficult to understand at first, but if we observe what we see in and around us, it becomes clear. We can choose to focus our awareness on beautiful sights, listen deeply to those who use thoughtful speech, and make a concentrated effort to embrace the gift of simplicity. Furthermore, each of us has the capacity not only for happiness, but also for bringing happiness to others. If humans are able to walk on this path together, it will be on account of our practice of *samtusta*, not on account of a rule of law or because of a divine commandment.

Some eight hundred years ago Francis of Assisi noted that what we own owns us. Those who have possessions are owned by their possessions. This seems unavoidable, particularly to those who place little value or fail to give voice to their soul. The true goal of all religions is to lead us back to the place where everything is one, to the experience of radical unity with humanity, nature, and with God. Religion has no other purpose than to make possible this one journey. Such a journey is difficult to describe with words, for the crucial point is that it's my personal journey and your personal journey, a journey one must take individually.

Simplicity need not be defined in the negative—as a life free of craving, as self-denial, or even as sacrifice. Simplicity, properly understood, fills us with joy and happiness. According to the teachings of Buddhism, simplifying our lives allows us to look deeply into things. When we do, we discover the interdependence and impermanence of all things, the source of compassion.

2. Stillness: Just Listening

Henri Nouwen, the internationally renowned priest and author, underscored the primacy of stillness when he noted that "without solitude it is virtually impossible to live a spiritual life." According to the spiritual masters, stillness, the simple art of listening, is one of the most perfect forms of prayer is the simple art of listening. The psalmist put it well: "Be still, and know that I am God" (Ps. 46:10). Though we might never reach a time when we will not need to use prayerful words, we should gradually discover that the most perfect form of prayer is simply a silent and loving entertainment of divine presence in our lives. This mystical form of prayer, sometimes called Centering Prayer, will unite us with God but also, perhaps surprisingly, it will forge a bond of love and concern with all other human beings.[3]

Brian McLaren tells a story of Mother Teresa, who was asked by a reported what she said to God when she prayed. She replied, "Mostly I just listen." The reporter then asked what God said to her: "Mostly God just listens," she replied. This interchange prompted McLaren to ask, "Could it be that the loving, attentive, mutual listening of the soul and the Spirit constitute the greatest expression of spirituality?" Lovers know this to be true; they know there is a kind of "just listening" that is one of the highest expressions of love.

Holy listening holds space open between beloved and Beloved, the soul and God, and that space, like the silence in which music happens, holds infinite possibilities. This deep silence may not produce spiritual highs, but it yields beneficial fruit. According to Susan Muto, "Silence brings to our bodies the grace of relaxation, to our minds the benefit of increased attention. It makes possible thoughtful speech and leads to more reflective action. Most of all it enables us to be centered in God. Its practical implications for formation are obvious, since it is a founding principle of the spiritual life."[4]

3. Contemplation: Holy Silence

Jesus gave us a process, a way of hearing, a way to look past the world of appearances—a journey called contemplation. Contemplation is a way to hear with the Spirit and not with the head. Contemplation is the search for wide-open space, space broad enough for the head, the heart, the feelings, the subconscious, our memories, our intuitions, our whole body. We need a holistic place for hearing. Unlike Moses, the Buddha, and Muhammad, Jesus may not have had a plan of what the perfect human society was supposed to look like (even God's Kingdom, of which he spoke frequently, is not a human contrivance), but he quite definitely wanted his followers to establish communities in which people come before things. Modern societies follow a reverse premise: use people and love things.

---

3. For additional information on the practice of Centering Prayer, consult Appendix B.

4. Muto, *Pathways of Spiritual Living*, 57–58.

Part III – The Second Half of Life

Richard Rohr provides a classic definition of contemplation, simple, direct, and beneficial: "Contemplation is a long, loving look at what really is."[5] The essential ingredient in this experience is time. We need to make time and identify a place where we can consider our lives comprehensively and anew. God has given us a spacious place within—a place we call soul. We journey inward not to become better people, or even to make ourselves holy; we go there to awaken.

Contemplation means returning to this deep source. Each of us has to find and commit to a spiritual exercise that helps us to come to this source. It can come by reading the Bible, through the sacraments, through prayer, or simply through silent meditation. But we must find a way to get to our center, where everything is. We have to take this long, loving look at reality, where we judge not but simply receive, for God is with us in that moment. Following the exercise, it is helpful to take a few minutes to assess the experience, trying to find a word or phrase for what happened during that moment.

Most people in the modern Western world have never really met the person they truly are, "the face they had before they were born," as Zen Buddhism puts it. The reason, at least in part, is because all through our lives we have been identifying either with our thoughts, our self-image, or our feelings. We have to find a way to get behind our thoughts, feelings, and self-image. As Richard Rohr notes, the first goal of meditation is "to find out who we were all along in God before we did anything right or wrong."[6] That's why we have to return to the level where we simply "are," where we're naked, where we discover how inherently good we are and paradoxically how goodness is a totally unearned gift. The goal of all spirituality is that in the end the naked person stands before the naked God. The import ingredient is our nakedness.

The effect of contemplation, as of all holy silence, is not mystical bliss, but authentic action. If contemplation does not lead to genuine service, it remains self-indulgent. We are told that if we practice regularly, we will come to the inner place of compassion. Surely compassion is worth it all. That's the meaning behind Augustine' outrageous statement: "love God and do what you want!" "People who are living from a God-centered place instead of a self-centered place are dangerously free precisely because they

---

5. Rohr, *Simplicity*, 92.
6. Ibid., 94.

are tethered at the center."[7] We cannot address the issues of our day by just acting from inner motives. The only way to stand redemptively in solidarity with persons who are different from us is to find that cosmic center, that singularity of unity, which enables us to view reality from the standpoint of others. That is the biblical meaning of *metanoia*, translated as "conversion."

On the way to contemplation we are guided by the example of Jesus in the wilderness. We may not be led to fast for forty days, but we must make ourselves empty. Of course, emptiness in and of itself is not enough. The point of emptiness is to get our false ego out of the way so that the Real Self can flourish. As soon as we are empty, we make room for Christ.

Long before dawn, according to Mark 1:35, Jesus went apart to a lonely place to pray. He went to the wilderness at the start of his ministry, and to the wilderness he returned, not only to pray, but to escape the demands of the madding crowds. We too, when we seek solitude, must depart from mundane routines, going into the wilderness for sustenance. In doing so we discover that our lives are not fully under our control. The thought of control in a wilderness seems ludicrous. This realization leads us to encounter a higher power, the mystery of God's will, to which we must surrender. In this way we move from the desperation of self-control to the delight of divine control, the delight of letting-go and letting-God.

Going to the wilderness evokes the mercy of God. In the desert God cannot help but respond to our needs and requests. By the same token, we can be more compassionate to ourselves and to others. In stillness we hear more deeply, to God's call in a sick parent, a confused student, a lonely stranger. Because God is patient with us, we begin to overcome our impatience with others, expressing greater care and compassion, working with greater passion but worrying less. With God's help, we can use our creative talents more fully while tolerating our limits.

In our practice, we need to distinguish between ardor and order. We are not serving routine; rather routine serves us. If a spiritual exercise teaches us nothing, then move on to something else. If the only person who prays well is the one who prays often, then the only person who contemplates well is the one who contemplates regularly. Emptiness cultivates fertile soil where we can be receptive to the seed of the Spirit. God may not dump the harvest into our lap, but God demonstrates the process of growth. In contemplation God provides us a way to listen and to forgive,

---

7. Ibid., 99.

and that way is through self-surrender. Ultimately, all spirituality is about letting go. Every contemplative teacher affirms this teaching.

When Carl Jung was an old man, one of his followers read John Bunyan's *Pilgrim's Progress* and he asked Jung, "What has your pilgrimage really been?" Jung replied: "My journey consisted in climbing down ten thousand ladders so that now at the end of my life I can extend the hand of friendship to this little clod of earth that I am." Such a reply can only be made by a person who is free. If we know that we are God's creatures, that we come from God and return to God, that is enough.

That is what happens when we expose ourselves to silence and stop exposing ourselves to the judgments of the world; when we stop relying on the energy of other humans; when we stop thinking about what others think of us and what they take us to be. We are who we are in God—no more and no less. That's why we have to go into the wilderness, guided by name to a deeper place. Here we will find the peace that the world cannot give, because we will discover what we have always been in God.

Less is more. Only those who have nothing to prove and nothing to protect, those who have enough space in them to embrace every part of their own soul, can receive the gift of silence. When we get to this place, we will know and love ourselves, in spite of negative and opposing evidence. It is the spacious place of the soul. To live there is to be at home. God is also at home there, and when we return we will have achieved the final goal of silence and simplicity.

4. Study: Reading Verbally and Nonverbally

In *Celebration of Discipline*, Richard Foster identifies twelve disciplines that may be practiced to achieve liberation from obsession to the false ego. He divides the disciplines into three categories as follows:

A. The Inward Disciplines: meditation, prayer, fasting, and study

B. The Outward Disciplines: simplicity, solitude, submission, and service

C. The Corporate Disciplines: confession, worship, guidance, and celebration

I find it fascinating that "study" is included in this distinguished list of disciplines. Given my profession, the discipline of study is essential in my life. By study I do not refer merely to scholarly activity, however, for the ultimate goal of the discipline of study is not factual or informational, but rather the renewal of the mind. Foster's understanding of study is expansive, for it includes verbal and nonverbal observation. By nonverbal he includes the study of nature, people, and events. Using this broad definition, each of us can and should be engaged daily in the discipline of study. If knowledge is related to truth, and "knowing the truth makes us free" (John 8:32), then study complements meditation, silence, and simplicity.

When we read books, many of us have poor reading habits, if we read much at all. Study, however, is an exacting art, governed by three distinct "readings," which in time can be done concurrently. The first reading involves *understanding* a book, discerning what the author is saying. The second reading involves *interpreting* the book, determining the author's meaning. The third reading involves *evaluating* the book, agreeing or disagreeing with its message. Such principles for reading encourage depth of involvement and understanding, essential to personal and spiritual growth. Effective reading also requires time, solitude, and reflection.

In reading scripture, a vast difference exists between the study of scripture and the devotional reading of scripture. In the study of scripture a high priority is placed upon interpretation; what it means. Devotional reading places high priority upon application: what it means to me. All too often people rush to the application stage and bypass the interpretation stage. Each approach is distinct, but both are necessary.

Study also includes observing nature, appreciating it, interacting with birds and flowers and streams, going for walks deep into the woods or high up the mountains, but stopping along the way to look and listen. Such experiences are therapeutic, for they enhance our connectedness with all that is. In *The Brothers Karamazov* Dostoyevsky counsels: "Love all God's creation, the whole and every grain of sand in it. Love every leaf, every ray of God's light. Love the animals, love the plants, love everything. If you love everything, you will perceive the divine mystery in things."

True spirituality begins with love of self (self-affirmation) and then proceeds to love of nature and love of others. The progression may not be the same for everyone, but all three are interrelated.

5. Stamina: Embracing Life with Passion and Enthusiasm

When I speak of stamina, I think of vitality of spirit, a constancy that fuels commitment. Such vitality is related to physical stamina and positive mental attitudes. Spirituality deals with the totality of life, the ins and outs and ups and downs of life, but when one encounters spirit as its depth, one is energized and renewed.

Part III – The Second Half of Life

To have passion is to have direction; to lose passion is to be adrift. Passion is essential for life, serving the life force (Eros). But passion cannot be limited to the physical, mental, or emotional realms. The soul desires ever-greater life, and what it desires may have little to do with our ego's schemes. The soul will lead us to places of spiritual risk and psychic danger—all in service to larger life. And for that we will need passion, spiritual stamina. The ultimate source of stamina is Spirit, renewed through silence, simplicity, study, and service. We are reminded yet again of Jung's central question: "Am I related to something infinite or not?" That relationship is the ultimate source of stamina.

6. Service: Practicing the Presence of God

The classic spiritual journey always begins elitist and ends egalitarian.
—KEN WILBER

Christian service involves two interrelated dimensions: love of God, manifested in worship, and love of neighbor, manifested in bringing joy to others and in addressing human need.

To worship is to experience God, and to experience God is to love and serve others. In the words of Brian McLaren, "There is nothing more radically activist than a truly spiritual life, and there is nothing more truly spiritual than a radically activist life."[8] Worship can be corporate, or it can be individual. Brother Lawrence experienced the presence of God in the kitchen, though he knew he could meet God in the Mass as well. In his classic work, *The Practice of the Presence of God*, Lawrence writes: "I cannot imagine how religious persons can live satisfied without the practice of the presence of God."

In contrast to the religions of the East, the Christian faith strongly emphasizes corporate worship. When Christians meet together, they often sense a profound unity, something they call *koinonia*, a deep inward fellowship in the power of the Spirit. One reason worship is a spiritual discipline is because it is an ordered way of living that gathers the faithful together so that God can transform them. True worship, then, is less an individual act and more a lifestyle. William Temple, Archbishop of Canterbury, defined worship as comprising a vast array of spiritual practices, including confession,

---

8. McLaren, *Naked Spirituality*, 237.

contemplation, meditation, invocation, and surrender: "To worship is to quicken the conscience by the holiness of God, to feed the mind with the truth of God, to purge the imagination by the beauty of God, to open the heart to the love of God, to devote the will to the purpose of God."

7. Enlightenment: Compassionate Living

The experience of the historical Buddha models our understanding of life as compassionate service. Buddhism presents the Buddha (Siddhartha Gautama) as a type rather than as an individual. After his enlightenment, we get no sense of his preferences, dislikes, hopes, or fears. The Buddha, we are told, was trying to find a new way of being human, a way characterized by serenity, equanimity, and profound self-control. While the Buddha's teachings are paradigmatic, equally illustrative are the events that led to his enlightenment.

Buddhist scriptures evolved elaborate mythological accounts of Siddhartha's renunciation of domesticity, including his going forth into homelessness. We are told that when Siddhartha was five days old, his father invited fortunetellers to a feast, where they could examine the infant and foretell his future. The Brahmins concluded that the child had a glorious future: he would become an enlightened spiritual leader or a heroic ruler.

Siddhartha's father, himself a king, deciding his son would become a monarch, confined him to a pleasure-palace existence, insulating him from negative influences or harsh realities. The young Siddhartha lived in a delusion, since his vision of the world did not coincide with reality. In his late twenties he experienced a deep discontent with his superficial conditions, which resulted in a complete break with his past. Venturing beyond his confinement, he witnessed four sights that transformed his perspective and his way of life. The "four sights" were of old age, sickness, death, and finally, of a monk whose withdrawal represented detachment from the world. Having opened up to universal suffering, his search for meaning could begin. His quest would not be easy; self-renunciation rarely is.

Renouncing his former life as misguided, Siddhartha set off to find a teacher who could instruct him in the path to enlightenment. During the next three years Siddhartha concentrated fully on his goal. He experimented with many approaches to spirituality, excelling in all but finding them deficient. At first he learned a great deal from his Hindu masters, mastering the essential disciplines, even superseding his teachers in their practice. Before long he concluded that he had learned all that these yogis could teach him. Besides, the teachings remained impractical abstractions, seemingly unrelated to his life. Even his teachers admitted they had not achieved the "direct knowledge" Gautama sought.

He then joined a band of ascetics, following the path of discipline and self-renunciation in order to achieve his goals. But this path only weakened him, resulting in near death. Asceticism proved as fruitless as yoga. But Gautama did not lose hope. He still believed that it was possible for human beings to reach the final liberation of enlightenment. Henceforth he would rely solely on his own insights—and on personal experience. Letting go of cherished dogmas, opinions, and related disciplines, he sat down under an old tree, near a riverbank, where "the beginning of a new solution declared itself to him."[9] Instead of torturing his reluctant self into the final release, he achieved enlightenment in seclusion, effortlessly and spontaneously. It was the moment of his awakening.

What produced this sudden change of perspective, later labeled the Middle Way (between the extremes of asceticism and indulgence)? It wasn't effort, diligence, or perseverance. Those had proven futile. He had, of course, previously committed himself to the "five prohibitions," moral preliminaries that considered as "unhelpful" activities such as violence, lying, stealing, intoxication, and illicit sex. But now, he realized these were not enough. He must cultivate the positive attitudes that were the opposite of these constraints. Later labeled "The Five Precepts of Buddhism," these behavioral guidelines were believed to encompass the highest form of prayer. *Ahimsa* (nonviolence) could only take one part of the way. Instead of simply avoiding violence, an aspirant must cultivate reverence for life (disinterested compassion), behaving gently and calmly with everything and everyone. It was important not to tell lies, but it was crucial to engage in "right talk," making sure that every word spoken was clear and beneficial. Besides refraining from stealing, individuals should take delight in living simply, cultivating good health by abstaining from intoxicants (by practicing mindful consumption). In Buddhism, abstaining from intoxicants involves refraining from meaningless consumption of food, drugs, or any product that contains toxins, including electronic websites, gambling, television programs, films, literature, and conversation.

Once this "skillful means" became habitual, Gautama believed, practitioners would "feel within pure joy," experiencing the divine directly in the present moment, a blissful mental, spiritual, and physical state he would

---

9. Armstrong, *Buddha*, 65.

later call "nirvana." By resolving to abandon the physical and emotional self-indulgence of his youth and the demanding idealistic path of self-improvement and perfectionism of his young adulthood, the Buddha came to experience for himself what no one else could teach him. "He resolved from then on to work with human nature and not to fight against it—amplifying states of mind that were conducive to enlightenment and turning his back on anything that would stunt his potential."[10]

First, as preliminary to meditation, came the practice that he called "mindfulness," living fully in the moment, appreciating its present potential. Initially this meant scrutinizing his behavior at every moment of the day, becoming mindful of his response to any ebb and flow of his feelings and sensations. This practice was not cultivated neurotically, but only as a means to full awareness. The Buddha noted that once distractions were named, they would soon fade away.

Having become convinced that the problem of human suffering lay within himself, mindfulness made him more acutely aware of the pervasiveness both of suffering and the desire that gave rise to it. Awareness of the short duration of his thoughts and longing led to the realization that everything was impermanent. If that were true, he concluded, why cling to objects or to cherished opinions as though they were permanent? This understanding led him to the principle of interbeing and interdependence, based on the unity of all things. If we observe things around us, we find that nothing comes from nothing. Before its so-called birth, a flower already existed in other forms—clouds, sunshine, seed, soil, and other elements. Later on, after its so-called death, the flower's constituents are transformed into other elements, like compost and soil. Interbeing is also interpenetration, because everything contains everything else. Each thing depends on all other things to be. Nothing can exist alone. It has to inter-be with all other things.

Longing for pleasure and permanence are also flawed, the Buddha realized, because they often result in suffering for others. Mindfulness made Gautama highly sensitive to the prevalence of the desire or craving that causes this suffering. Our view of the world, he taught, is distorted by greed, which often leads to ill-will and envy. When one's desires clash with the cravings of others, we often find ourselves filled with envy, hatred, and anger. Such states of mind are "unskillful" because they increase our own suffering, selfishness, and discontent.

10. Ibid., 71.

Part III – The Second Half of Life

In the Buddha's system, meditation would take the place of traditional worship, including the place of sacrifice. Likewise, compassion would replace asceticism. Once human beings cultivate friendship for everybody and everything, they can progress to true compassion, empathizing with others in their pain. Finally, humans can attain the state of contemplation, whereby they are so immersed in the object of their contemplation that they are beyond pain or pleasure. Gautama aspired to an attitude of total equanimity toward others, feeling neither attraction nor antipathy. This is a difficult state, since it requires that the practitioner divest completely of egotism, abandoning all personal preference in favor of disinterested benevolence. In his enlightenment, Gautama learned "to transcend himself in an act of total compassion toward all other beings, infusing the old disciplines with loving-kindness."[11]

If there is any truth to the story that Gautama gained enlightenment under the Bodhi tree, it could be that he acquired a sudden, absolute certainty that he had discovered a method that would bring an earnest seeker to nirvana. He never insisted that his method was new or an invention of his own. Rather he noted that he had simply discovered an ancient path that elucidated the fundamental principles that govern the life of the cosmos. His path was simply a statement of things "as they really are," a way written into the very structure of existence. If living beings kept to the path of interdependence, they could all attain a state that would bring them peace and fulfillment, because they no longer struggled against one another or their deepest grain.[12] When the Buddha achieved nirvana under the Bodhi tree, he did not shout "I am liberated," but "It is liberated." Having conquered the fires of greed, hatred, and delusion, he awakened to his full potential as a human being. He had found an inner realm of calm, thereby becoming a Buddha. However, he did not keep this to himself. He realized he must share his experience with others, for many in his world were longing for a new spiritual vision, a vision based on compassion. As the Buddha discovered, enlightened persons have not simply attained personal salvation, but have realized that to live morally is to live for others.

---

11. Ibid., 78.
12. Ibid., 82–83.

Desiderata

> Be the change you want to see in the world.
> —MOHANDAS GANDHI

RICHARD ROHR SPEAKS OF three ways of seeing: with the eye of the flesh (with the first eye, which is good), with the eye of reason (with the second eye, which is better), and with the eye of true understanding (with the third eye, which is best). If the first eye represents *sight* and *thought*, the second represents *meditation* or *reflection*, and the third represents *contemplation*, a way of seeing that leads to genuine encounter because it sees coherence, spaciousness, and underlying mystery.

The third eye—the mystical gaze—builds upon the first two ways of seeing, and yet goes further. It is a different way of knowing and touching the moment. This happens whenever body, mind, and heart awareness are simultaneously open and nonresistant. This is what Rohr calls "presence" or "being present." The experience of "presence," manifest in moments of deep inner connection, makes us want to write poetry, create music, pray, weep, or be utterly silent. Some call these moments "conversion," others "enlightenment," "transformation," or "holiness."

Third-eye persons have been saints, seers, poets, metaphysicians, or authentic mystics—gifted individuals who have "moved from mere belief systems or belonging systems to actual inner experience."[1] This experience was Paul's "third heaven," when "he heard things that are not to be told, that no moral is permitted to repeat" (2 Cor. 12:4). Consciously or not, too much organized religion has kept us in the first or second heaven, seeing with the first or second eye, where all can be articulated with proper lan-

---

1. Rohr, *Naked Now*, 29–30.

guage and where doctrine is deemed certain. The reasons for this may or may not be intentional, but rather may be due to a third possibility, namely that one can lead people only as far as one has gone.

An enormous breakthrough occurs when we honor and accept the divine image within ourselves, for we cannot help but see it in others as well, knowing it is just as undeserved as it is in us. That is when we stop judging and how we start loving unconditionally.

You may have heard the expression, "What you see is what you get." That axiom is as true spiritually as it is in other realms of life. The image of God in you calls forth the image of love in others. Wholeness sees and calls forth wholeness in others. Unconditional love in you calls forth unconditional love in others.

Another axiom holds equally true; "What you seek is what you get." If we want others to be more loving, choose to love first; if we seek peace in the outer world, we must create it inside first; if we seek a just world, we must start being just ourselves. As Rohr exhorts: "If you want to find God, then honor God within you, and you will always see God beyond you. For it is only God in you who knows where and how to look for God."[2]

While some people liken the second-half-of-life journey to one's religious or faith conversion, for me they are related but distinct. Unlike persons who have had a recognizable "conversion" experience, dated to a specific event or set of events, for me the second-half journey has come in stages and culminated in a new sense of calling or vocation as a Christian.

Whereas to this point my faith journey/way of life has comprised cumulative and progressive insights and perspectives, retirement allows me to embody my second journey through a fresh start, new goals, and different priorities, resulting in a new sensibility and an altered lifestyle. Whereas in the past I saw my Christian calling as a quest for certainty, competence, and consistency, supported by a set of spiritual disciplines that required both start-up and renewed effort to accomplish, I now see my calling as relinquishing competence, certainty, and other forms of human effort in order to simply "abide" in God through Christ and the Holy Spirit (John 15:4–5).

At this moment this implies significant changes pedagogically and spiritually, including (1) that I no longer teach courses that are content-driven or coercive in style, where I am viewed as the "expert"; (2) that I give up apologetic activities designed to bring others to a "correct"

2. Ibid., 161.

understanding of God, Christ, the Holy Spirit, scripture, or faith; and (3) that I renounce activities or attitudes that are merely extensions of what my ego might consider to be true; (4) that I refrain from participating in debates, competitions, or other events that might show me to be right and, by implication, others to be wrong, and (5) that I refrain from activities that are demeaning or disrespectful of others. (6) The only forms of witness or evangelism I wish to observe are those that come through actions and lifestyle. (7) My worship, while occasionally expressed corporately, will focus on meditation/contemplation and on what John's Gospel calls foot-washing (i.e. service to others; see 13:1–16). (8) Finally, I will avoid invitations to preach in churches or at gatherings where I am put on a pedestal and viewed as a dispenser of truth. I will take as motto the words of 1Timothy 6:6–7: "Religion yields high dividends, but only to the person whose resources are within. We brought nothing into the world, and we cannot take anything with us when we leave, but if we have food and clothing we may rest content" (NEB).

My mentor is Jesus, who gave up equality with God, adopting the lifestyle of a servant. Joining the "dispossessed" (see Matt. 5:3; Luke 6:20), he humbled himself, exchanging one form of glory for another. My exemplars are the Johannine Peter and the Beloved Disciple, the yin and yang of early Christian discipleship, polar opposites though forever paired in paradigmatic unity: Peter, appointed shepherd of the flock and charged to witness through martyrdom and death (see John 21:18–19); the Beloved Disciple, appointed teacher of the flock and charged to witness through longevity and life (see John 21:20–24).

Will the changes I seek take hold or last forever? I do not know, for I am no longer in charge.

APPENDIX A

Qualities of the Second-Half Journey

BELOW IS A PARTIAL list of benefits—gifts really—that characterize second-half persons. Feel free to include additional qualities that you have observed in others or experienced yourself.

1. Redefined belief systems; emphasis on inner rather than outer truth
2. Greater self-acceptance
3. Greater tolerance for uncertainty and ambiguity
4. Living happily within one's limits and circumstances
5. Acceptance of pain, suffering, and death
6. Greater service to others
7. Becoming an agent of health, healing, and wholeness
8. Enhanced vision for self and society
9. Living, thinking, and acting mindfully
10. Awareness of impermanence
11. Awareness of interdependence (non-dualistic thinking)
12. Living holistically: alignment of body and mind with soul and spirit
13. Direct encounter with the Divine (finding God in oneself and oneself in God)
14. Awareness of one's powers of presence and wonder
15. Awareness and sensitivity to one's "longings"
16. Enhanced risk-taking ability
17. Compassionate living; loving unselfishly

18. Acceptance of change (becoming an agent of transformation and change)
19. Living more simply, with less complication, tension, and stress
20. Greater patience
21. Greater generosity
22. Being less dogmatic and less opinionated
23. Being less competitive and less argumentative
24. Enhanced conviction and commitment

APPENDIX B

Practicing Presence: Helpful Methods

THIS SEGMENT PROVIDES READERS with useful advice on two of the most ancient and universal spiritual practices for encountering Christ: Centering Prayer and Lectio Divina. The immediate and obvious effect of these practices is to transform the way one thinks, breaking the tyranny of the mind, with its compulsive thinking. Their underlying effect is to provide practitioners with a direct experience of being itself, unmediated by thinking but rather by heart perception.

Centering Prayer

Meditation practices come in a variety of forms, each with its own particular way of quieting the ordinary mind and taking you deeper into being. If you have a meditational practice already, I encourage you to stay with it. But if not, or if for some reason the practices you have tried haven't stuck, I invite you to use a method called Centering Prayer. This tradition does not focus on the mind but rather goes straight for the heart. Simply put, it is a method of surrender, a practice based entirely on letting go of thoughts as they arise. The intention is to lead you to that place where, as Paul puts it, the Spirit prays within you, for God searches the heart, and the Spirit knows what is in your heart (Rom. 8:26–27).

Centering Prayer is a daily practice of sitting in silence and becoming aware of God's presence in our lives. It is a method of prayer that does not include words or scripture reading. Instead, it is the opening of our mind and heart, our whole being, to God through silence. The first point to keep in mind in the practice of Centering Prayer is intention. To the extent that your intention is clear and strong, your practice will be also. If your intention gets muddled and confused, so will your practice. If your aim is to make yourself empty or still, you will soon give up or go on to other things.

However, if your intention is to be deeply present, that is, to be available to God, at one with that mysterious presence at the depths of your being, then you can let go of all attachment to outcome and simply stay quiet and available.

The method for the practice of Centering Prayer is simple. Once you have gotten into a comfortable position, a short scripture reading or prayer can help prepare the way. Because the mind is prone to wandering, Centering Prayer recommends the use of a short word or phrase that symbolizes your consent to God's presence and action within. Common choices are *Jesus*, *God*, *Spirit*, or *Love*, or meaningful foreign words like *pax*, *agape*, or *shalom*. Close your eyes and then repeat the sacred word silently. When a thought arises and you become aware of it, simply release the thought, return to the sacred word, and start over. You are neither denying the thought nor trying not to think, only letting it come and go. This minimum of effort is the only real activity of Centering Prayer. After repeating the sacred word several times at the beginning and throughout the practice, you may find that the word will drop out on its own. Like falling asleep at night, you will eventually lose track of the moment when it happens. It will only return when you start thinking again. At such times simply use your sacred word to let go of the thought and return to silence.

The basic practice lasts twenty to thirty minutes, at which time slowly open your eyes and take a few minutes to return to your usual state of consciousness. These few moments of transition are important, allowing you to savor the experience and take its energy with you into your ordinary activities. Keep in mind that Centering Prayer is not about having great mystical experiences; it is about practicing presence, no matter what the subjective experience may be. Meditational practices that seem the hardest may well be the ones where the most inner ground is being gained.[1]

Lectio Divina

Another meditational practice with a long history of practice in the Christian tradition is called Lectio Divina, is a simple yet profound way of praying the scriptures that transcends mental processing. Those who utilize this approach today emphasize a meditative, not a scholarly or literary approach, with the intention of learning what God has to say to us about the true meaning of life for themselves and for the world. In Lectio

---

1. Bourgeault, *Wisdom Jesus*, 148.

Practicing Presence: Helpful Methods

Divina one works intensely with a short scriptural passage following four distinct steps called *lectio* (reading), *meditatio* (reflection), *oratio* (prayer), and *contemplatio* (contemplation). While these steps are usually presented as sequential, experienced practitioners often experience them as circular, with the steps unfolding in any order.

Following this method, participants are encouraged to select a text, reading it slowly and attentively. If they wish, they may pause for a moment of silence before reading the passage again. In the second step, known as *meditatio*, readers will engage with the text through focused mental reflection, using reason, imagination, memory, and emotions to work with the passage. The process may differ with each passage. Sometimes the passage may trigger a memory, or it might stimulate one's thinking or bring confusion. Or participants might be struck by a certain term, phrase, or compelling image. Another effective way of working with the text is to role play one of the characters. Whatever approach one uses, this is not biblical research. This practice is not about acquiring information or scholarly perspective. It is about allowing the text to resonate with one's own heart.

The third stage, *oratio*, encourages heart-to-heart encounter with scripture. As feelings arise, participants ponder them quietly, insightfully. If possible, feelings can be shaped into a prayer, using words of petition, gratitude, or concern. This is the moment when, in Paul's words, the Spirit begins to pray within oneself. A prayer, of course, doesn't have to be in words; the feelings themselves can be the prayer. If the text causes no such response, participants are encouraged not to force a response but simply to move on to the next step.

The final step is known as *contemplatio*, which in the mystical tradition denotes "resting in God." At this stage one suspends all mental and emotional activity and simply "rests" in the fullness of the experience. As with Centering Prayer, the real work goes on beneath the level of one's conscious mind.

While *lectio*, *meditatio*, *oratio*, and *contemplatio* form the traditional sequence, experienced practitioners tend to follow the movement of the Spirit, weaving between the steps in a fluid way. Devoting half an hour a day to this practice, or even half an hour several times a week, will produce dramatic differences in one's intimacy level with scripture. Words and images that arise during one's time of *lectio* will percolate beneath the activities of one's day, shaping what one see and does in remarkable ways. Incidentally, the passage one reads need not be long. Some select a single sentence—even a single word—sometimes for days, until the text reveals its hidden treasure.

The question naturally arises as to where in the Bible one should begin to apply this method. While there is no correct answer to this question, two strategies are available. One is to pick a book of the Bible, such as the epistle of James, one of the gospels, or a short letter by Paul, and simply begin. The Psalms are a perennial rich ground for Lectio Divina, as are Old Testament wisdom books such as Proverbs or Ecclesiastes. If one works at this process long and patiently enough, one may eventually cover the entire Bible.

The other strategy is to work with what's known as the daily lectionary. Most of the mainstream Christian denominations (Roman Catholic, Episcopal, Lutheran, Presbyterian, Methodist, and United Church of Christ) make use of a standard set of readings for Sunday and daily devotional use.[2] For each day the lectionary provides several readings, including an Old Testament passage, an epistle and a gospel. One may choose any of these texts during their time of *lectio*, or else take the readings for the upcoming Sunday and work with them a bit at a time throughout the week: the gospel one day, the epistle the next, the Old Testament reading the next, or whatever approach one chooses. The daily readings expand the range of biblical reading in worship and personal devotion by providing daily citations for the full three-year cycle of the Revised Common Lectionary. These readings complement the Sunday and festival readings. Thursday through Saturday readings help prepare readers for the Sunday ahead; Monday through Wednesday readings help readers reflect on what they heard in worship the previous Sunday. Again, the passage one reads need not be long; it can be as short as a verse or even a single sentence or word.

While Lectio Divina is primarily done individually, group practice is becoming common. Group *lectio* can indeed be a powerful experience and a natural complement to group Centering Prayer. When practiced in a group setting, this exercise is very different from a Bible study group, for leaders and practitioners are not there to share or discuss or debate. A good way to proceed is to designate an appropriate leader, one who will adhere to the process. Following a period of silence, a designated person will read the scriptural passage, slowly and quietly. Before the actual reading, the leader should instruct each person to listen for the sentence, phrase, or even the single word that seems to call for attention. After a moment of

---

2. I recommend that you use the daily readings from the Revised Common Lectionary found online on the Vanderbilt Divinity library website.

silence, the passage should be read aloud again. Following this reading, the leader invites participants to speak aloud the word, phrase, or sentence that has moved them. Members of the group can be assured that repetition is appropriate, particularly since people often pick up different nuances in the text. After the exercise has run its course, the passage can be read a third time, followed by a return to silence for several minutes. The group leader may offer a closing prayer, after which the group leaves in silence.

While this group exercise focuses mainly on the first step of Lectio Divina, the silence between the readings provides participants space to engage in their own *meditatio* and *oratio*. Traditional fellowship and Bible study is well and good, but it tends to pull members back into their usual patterns of thinking, whereas this more contemplative approach carries people "beyond the mind" into the greater "heart knowing" we have been exploring throughout this book.

What begins to emerge in persons from the slow, patient work in Lectio Divina is not only an intimate familiarity with scripture but also a distinct relationship with the text described as the awakening of the unitive imagination, where "the poetry of scripture and the poetry of one's own life come together to form a single whole."[3]

---

3. Bourgeault, *Wisdom Jesus*, 160.

APPENDIX C

Walking the Wire: A Sermon

(Genesis 2:8-9, 15–17; 3:1–7, 22–24)

ON THE EVENING OF June 15, 2012, 33-year-old daredevil Nik Wallenda went for a 25-minute walk, becoming the first person to walk on a tightrope 1,800 feet across Niagara Falls (Horseshoe Falls), starting on the American side. A crowd of 4,000 people watched on the American side and 125,000 on the Canadian side, in addition to millions of TV viewers. Along the way, Nik prayed aloud. When customs agents asked him for his passport, which he presented, he was asked the purpose of his trip. Nik's response was classic: "I want to inspire people around the world."

This feat was the fulfillment of a lifelong dream as well as an opportunity to honor his great grandfather, the legendary Karl Wallenda, who died after falling from a tightrope in Puerto Rico in 1978, the year before Nik was born. When Nik Wallenda walked the high wire across the Niagara Falls, he was building on a family tradition that dates back centuries. Nik represents the seventh generation of the Flying Wallendas, a traveling family circus troupe that traces its history back to 1780s Europe. "People say I'm insane," he remarks, "but they don't understand this is something I've done since I was 2. It's just in my blood."

I would like to relate this illustration to our general human condition, building on the well-known account of the first humans found in Genesis 2 and 3, known ironically as the "Fall of Man." These chapters are one of the best known, yet most baffling portions of scripture. What are they about? Theologians and commentators differ widely on their interpretation. Are they about sexuality and the loss of innocence? About gaining a conscience? About moral knowledge, evil, or original sin?

Rather than focusing on the details of the account, as if it were an allegory, I would like to suggest that we examine one aspect of the story—the two trees in the Garden—and consider them as two types of existence possible for humans in a universe provided by God.

The first type of existence, symbolized by the Tree of Life, represents

a. Plateaued existence in a garden of bliss; a gilded-cage existence, somewhat like the pleasure-palace into which the young Siddartha (later to become the Buddha) was placed by his father so that he might control the destiny of his son and keep him on the path to becoming a powerful ruler rather than a compassionate healer;

b. a universe of aggressive Providence, where God is everywhere present and everywhere active.

Under the dynamics of a Tree of Life existence, the needs of humanity and the vicissitudes of nature are handled by a hands-on God, who like a helicopter parent hovers over humans as though they were infants in a comfortable home. All is lush and relatively problem-free. Human growth and dignity are sacrificed on the altar of bliss. All is taken care of.

By contrast, the second type of existence, symbolized by the Tree of Knowledge, represents a quite opposite set of dynamics, including:

a. a life of challenge, freedom of choice, and responsibility;

b. the reality of temptation;

c. an aggressive pursuit of knowledge;

d. pain and joy in great extremes;

e. a life of independence and risk;

f. mortality by virtue of natural and moral evil;

g. a higher potential for moral good and for moral evil;

h. diminished Divine Providence; and

i. the possibility of a lifestyle based on faith.

According to this scenario, human individualism, creativity, and capacities for good and for growth will have a greater arena for expression but so also human cruelty and natural calamity. By seeking to manage their environment and to nurture it, rather than to have it handed to them on a silver platter, humans living in the Tree of Knowledge type of existence come closer to a true image of God than they do in the Tree of Life scenario.

Walking the Wire: A Sermon

Biblical support for this understanding comes from the syntax of Genesis 2:9, where the phrase commonly translated as "and the tree of the knowledge of good and evil" literally reads: "and the Tree of Knowledge, (comma) good and evil," or it could very well be translated: "and the Tree of Knowledge; (semicolon) consequently good and evil."

So we have two ways of life; two complete sets of dynamics: the dynamics of the Tree of Life and the dynamics of the Tree of Knowledge. And these sets are mutually exclusive. One may not simultaneously operate under both sets of dynamics at the same time. One cannot possess full freedom and full knowledge. Nor can humans have the "best" elements of each set simultaneously. For example, according to the dynamics of the Tree of Knowledge, we cannot know ourselves fully or know God directly. Such universal truths are elements of the Tree of Life paradigm.

Perhaps that is the meaning, at least in part, of two of the Bible's great maxims:

a. "The secret things belong to the Lord our God; but the things that are revealed belong to us and to our children for ever" (Deuteronomy 29:29);

b. "Now I know in part; then I shall understand fully" (1 Corinthians 13:12).

According to this understanding of Genesis, it was actually humans who determined the expulsion from the Garden of Bliss, seeking the destiny of the Tree of Knowledge with all that the choice implies. Therefore, by choice and of necessity, humans no longer live in the Garden of Bliss, but rather East of Eden, where mortality and uncertainty but also faith and freedom dwell.

We have been taught that Adam and Eve sinned in partaking of the Tree of Knowledge and I would like to question that understanding. My interpretation is that while Adam and Eve acted contrary to divine caution, the category of classic "sin" here is not applicable. Rather Adam and Eve, the symbolic parents of humanity, exercised their divinely granted measure of freedom to decline the warning of the Divine, thereby choosing the path of dynamics known by the title "Tree of Knowledge." This high-risk approach to life, which humans embraced, may not have been favored by God, but it was definitely permitted. And the essential choice of that path, if one follows the story literally, was made by Eve, the mother of mankind. The one who bears the child and suffers the pain in childbirth chose to set her children along the more arduous, but hopefully more rewarding path of the Tree of Knowledge.

This approach raises the question of evil, suggesting that with the creation of potential for good—which is required for humans to reach their spiritual capacity—potential for evil indirectly came into existence as a consequence.

a. Perhaps this is what Augustine meant when he noted that "Evil has its source in the good";

b. and what Thomas Aquinas had in mind when he stated "There is no possible source of evil except good";

c. and what the author of Isaiah had in mind when he quotes God as saying: "I form light and create darkness, I make weal [Heb. peace or harmony] and create woe [the Hebrew word here is the word for evil found in Genesis 2: 9 and is translated thus by the authors of the KJV], I the Lord do all these things" (45:7).

The reference to evil in Isaiah undoubtedly has in mind the destruction of the Temple in Jerusalem by the Babylonians in the sixth century BC and the ensuing Exile. However, in Jewish tradition, omnipotent God is constrained from destroying evil for by doing so God could well destroy good. While an omnipotent Deity could violate universal laws, to do so might unravel the cosmos.

These views represent consistent and classical monotheism, refreshing in the light of the rampant dualism that characterizes the mindset of many contemporary Christians, Muslims, and other so-called monotheists.

One last principle needs to be mentioned about the two trees in the Garden, namely that the two sets of dynamics they represent are in inverse proportion. The more one increases the influence and magnitude of elements inherent in one set, the more one decreases the influence and magnitude of the dynamics inherent in the other set. Those who embrace the security and certainty of the Tree of Life paradigm, including a full and aggressive Divine Providence, decrease the elements of the Tree of Knowledge paradigm—including the elements of challenge, freedom, and responsibility. Those who embrace the Tree of Knowledge way of life choose freedom and responsibility but also risk and uncertainty. The expansion of one set implies the contraction of the other.

In the concluding book of the Bible, the author of the book of Revelation illustrates this point when, in describing the new Paradise, the Heavenly

Jerusalem, in chapter 22, there is no mention of the Tree of Knowledge but only of the Tree of Life. Only at the end, in this final paradigm, is there no night, no mortality, no illness, and no evil, but only the set of dynamics implicit in the Tree of Life option.

Those of us who live here and now, according to the dynamics of what we have called The Tree of Knowledge—and that would be all of us—must exchange that final certainty, security, and bliss ("walking by sight") for uncertainty and insecurity ("walking by faith"). On at least the level of faith, I encourage you to join the Flying Wallendas, to become tightrope walkers.

When Nik Wallenda walked the tightrope across the Horseshoe Falls on June 15, 2012, all the dynamics of the Tree of Knowledge type of existence came into play. He was taking a huge risk; the conditions were treacherous, and there were no guarantees of success. But three factors were in his favor:

1. Tradition: he was backed by the wisdom and experience of generations of ancestors;
2. Safety harness: he was tethered to the wire, supported by a security system that he could count on if the unpredictable winds and the misty conditions proved to be overwhelming;
3. Balancing pole; he carried a balance beam attached by a brace to his neck to keep him grounded, focused, and stable.

Without these three, he would have been unable to cross the wire to the other side.

So it is in our lives: as we walk the tightrope of our earthly existence, we find we must leave the security and safety of the Garden of our infancy and walk the tightrope of life, heading across the gorge to the other side. And we will make it safely to our destination if by faith we keep moving, simply placing one foot in front of the other, focusing on the goal before us, and relying on three factors:

1. Our faith tradition, a 2,000-year-old tradition of tightrope walking known as the Christian Church;
2. The person of Jesus, the pioneer of all our tightrope-walking efforts;
3. And the balance beam of scripture and worship, which keep us grounded and balanced in life.

And as we do, let us rely on the primary promise of that scripture, made by Jesus, the pioneer of walking by faith, when he assured his disciples: "I am with you always, wherever you go, and I will never leave you nor forsake you."

Bibliography

Armstrong, Karen. *Buddha*. New York: Viking, 2001.
Barnhart, Bruno. *The Future of Wisdom*. New York: Continuum, 2007.
———. *Second Simplicity*. Mahwah, NJ: Paulist, 1999.
Barton, Ruth Haley. *Invitation to Solitude and Silence*. Downers Grove, IL: InterVarsity, 2004.
Bourgeault, Cynthia. *The Wisdom Jesus*. Boston: Shambhala, 2008.
———. *The Wisdom Way of Knowing*. San Francisco: Jossey-Bass, 2003
Chopra, Deepak. *How to Know God*. New York: Three Rivers, 2000.
Dumm, Demetrius. *Praying the Scriptures*. Collegeville, MN: Liturgical Press, 2003.
Foster, Richard J. *Celebration of Discipline*. Rev. ed. San Francisco: HarperSanFrancisco, 1988.
Fowler, James. *Stages of Faith: The Psychology of Human Development and the Quest for Meaning*. San Francisco: HarperSanFrancisco, 1995.
Fox, Matthew. *Original Blessing*. Santa Fe, NM: Bear & Co., 1983.
Fromm, Eric. *The Art of Loving*. New York: Harper & Row, 1956.
Hanh, Thich Nhat. *Good Citizens*. Berkeley, CA: Parallax, 2012.
———. *Living Buddha, Living Christ*. Rev. ed. New York: Riverhead, 2007.
———. *The Miracle of Mindfulness: An Introduction to the Practice of Meditation*. Translated by Mobi Ha. Boston: Beacon, 1976.
Hollis, James. *Finding Meaning in the Second Half of Life: How to Finally, Really Grow Up*. New York: Gotham, 2006.
———. *The Middle Passage: From Misery to Meaning in Midlife*. Toronto: Inner City Books, 1993.
Homes, Urban T. *The History of Christian Spirituality*. New York: Seabury, 1980.
Johnson, Robert. *Transformation: Understanding the Three Levels of Masculine Consciousness*. San Francisco: HarperSanFrancisco, 1991.
Jones, Alan. *Journey into Christ*. New York: Seabury, 1977.
Katie, Byron. *A Thousand Names for Joy: Living in Harmony with the Way Things Are*. New York: Harmony, 2007.
———. *Loving What Is: Four Questions That Can Change Your Life*. New York: Three Rivers, 2002.
Keirsey, David, and Marilyn Bates. *Please Understand Me: Character & Temperament Types*. Del Mar, CA: Prometheus Nemesis, 1978.
Lane, Belden. *The Solace of Fierce Landscaper: Exploring Desert and Mountain Spirituality*. New York: Oxford University Press, 1998.

Bibliography

Lawrence, Gordon. *People Types & Tiger Stripes*. Gainsville, FL: Center for Application of Psychological Type, 1979.

Leech, Kenneth. *True Prayer*. Harrisburg, PA: Morehouse, 1995.

Lesser, Elizabeth. *The Seeker's Guide: Making Your Life a Spiritual Adventure*. New York: Villard, 2000.

Levinson, Daniel. *The Season of a Man's Life*. New York: Knopf, 1978.

McLaren, Brian D. *A Generous Orthodoxy*. Grand Rapids, MI: Zondervan, 2004.

———. *A New Kind of Christianity: Ten Questions That Are Transforming the Faith*. New York: HarperCollins, 2010.

———. *Naked Spirituality*. San Francisco: HarperOne, 2011.

Merton, Thomas. *Contemplative Prayer*. New York: Herder and Herder, 1969.

———. *Thoughts in Solitude*. Garden City, NY: Image Books, 1968.

Moore, Thomas. *Care of the Soul: A Guide for Cultivating Depth and Sacredness in Everyday Life*. New York: HarperPerennial, 1994.

Muto, Susan Annette. *Pathways of Spiritual Living*. Petersham, MA: St. Bede's, 1984.

Myers, Isabel Briggs, with Peter B. Myers. *Gifts Differing: Understanding Personality Type*. Palo Alto, CA: Davies-Black, 1980.

Norberg, Tilda. *The Chocolate-Covered Umbrella: Discovering Your Dreamcode*. Nashville: Fresh Air Books, 2008.

———. *Consenting to Grace*. Staten Island, NY: Gestalt Pastoral Care, 1996

Palmer, Helen. *The Enneagram: Understanding Yourself and the Others in Your Life*. San Francisco: HarperSanFrancisco, 1991.

Peck, M. Scott. *The Different Drum*. New York: Simon & Schuster, 1987.

Plotkin, Bill. *Nature and the Human Soul: Cultivating Wholeness and Community in a Fragmented World*. Novato, CA: New World Library, 2008.

———. *Soulcraft: Crossing into Mysteries of Nature and Psyche*. Novato, CA: New World Library, 2003.

Raguin, Yves. *Paths to Contemplation*. St. Meinrad, IN: Abbey, 1974.

Richardson, Peter Tufts. *Four Spiritualities*. Palo Alto, CA: Davies-Black, 1996.

Rohr, Richard. *Falling Upward: A Spirituality for the Two Halves of Life*. San Francisco: Jossey-Bass, 2011.

———. *The Naked Now: Learning to See as the Mystics See*. New York: Crossroad, 2009.

———. *Simplicity: The Freedom of Letting Go*. New York: Crossroad, 2004.

Smith, Huston. *Forgotten Truth: The Common Vision of the World's Religions*. San Francisco: HarperSanFrancisco, 1992 (1976).

———. *The World's Religions*. Rev. 2nd ed. San Francisco: HarperSanFrancisco, 1991.

Stein, Murray. *In Midlife: A Jungian Perspective*. Dallas: Spring Publications, 1994.

Thompson, Marjorie J. *Soul Feast: An Invitation to the Christian Spiritual Life*. Louisville, KY: Westminster John Knox, 1995.

Tolle, Eckhart. *The Power of Now*. Novato, CA: New World Library, 2004

Vande Kappelle. Robert. *Beyond Belief: Faith, Science, and the Value of Unknowing*. Eugene: OR: Wipf & Stock, 2012.

———. *Iron Sharpens Iron: A Discussion Guide for Twenty-First-Century Seekers*. Eugene, OR: Wipf & Stock, 2013.

———. *Truth Revealed: The Message of the Gospel of John—Then and Now*. Eugene, OR: Wipf & Stock, 2014.

———. *Wisdom Revealed: The Message of Biblical Wisdom Literature—Then and Now*. Eugene, OR: Wipf & Stock, 2014.

Bibliography

Westerhoff, John. *Spiritual Life: The Foundation for Preaching and Teaching*. Louisville, Westminster John Knox, 1994.
Whyte, David. *The Three Marriages: Reimagining Work, Self and Relationship*. New York: Riverhead, 2009.
Wilber, Ken, et al. *Integral Life Practice*. Boston: Integral Books, 2008.
———. *Integral Spirituality: A Startling New Role for Religion in the Modern and Postmodern World*. Boston: Shambhala, 2006.
———. *The Simple Feeling of Being: Embracing Your True Nature*. Boston: Shambhala, 2004.
Wilber, Ken, Jack Engler, and Daniel Brown. *Transformations of Consciousness: Conventional and Contemplative Perspectives on Development*. Boston: New Science Library, 1986.
Yancey, Philip. *Prayer: Does It Make Any Difference?* Grand Rapids, MI: Zondervan, 2006.

Subject/Name Index

Abraham, 72–75, 81
Adickes, Erich, 42
adolescence, 4, 7, 9, 12, 14, 15, 17, 18, 19, 69, 83, 84–87
ahimsa (nonviolence), 120
Aquinas, Thomas, 20, 138
Aristotle, 42
Augustine, 33, 91–92, 114, 138

Barth, Karl, xi
Beloved Disciple, 75, 125
Blake, William, 61
body. *See* physical body
Brother Lawrence, 118
Buddha, 32, 113, 119–22
Buddhism, 61, 66, 111–12, 114, 120
Bunyan, John, 116

Christology, 90–91
compassion, 62, 112, 114, 115, 122, 127
contemplation, 58, 59, 61, 113–16, 122, 123, 131
contemplative (centering) prayer, 52, 113, 129–30
conversion (*metanoia*), 115, 123, 124

Dalai Lama, xvi
D'Arcy, Paula, 100
Dostoyevsky, Feodor, 117
dreams, x, xvii–xix, 6, 78, 85, 86
dualistic/nondualistic thought, 20, 61, 90–91, 99–100, 103, 110
Dumm, Demetrius, 55

ego/false ego, 15–16, 66, 71, 75, 77, 78, 81, 82, 85, 104, 110

egocentric, 17, 69, 81, 84
Einstein, Albert, 76
elderhood, 84, 96, 97
election, 72
Eliot, T. S., 95, 108
enlightenment, 119–22, 123
Enneagram, 46–49
Erikson, Erik, 7–10
Eucharist, 56–58
Evagrius of Pontus, 47
evil, 138–39
Eysenck, Hans, 42

faith, 72, 73–74, 106
Fall of Man, 135–38
false ego. *See* ego
fear, xx
first half of life, ix, x, xv, 65–75, 81, 84, 85–86, 98, 106–7
Foster, Richard, xiv, 116
Fourth Way, 47
Fowler, James, 13–15
Fox, Matthew, xiv, 5
Francis of Assisi, 81, 112
Fromm, Eric, 42

Galen, 41
Gandhi, Mohandas, 123
Gestalt Pastoral Care, 49–50
God, xvi, 21, 89, 90, 92
    experiences of, x, 51, 54–62, 106, 114, 118, 124
    faith journey and, 4, 116
    images of, xi, 72, 91–92
Grant, W. Harold, 83
Gregory of Nyssa, 72

145

Subject/Name Index

Gurdjieff, George, 46–48

Hanh, Thich Nhat, xiv, 61
heaven, 88, 89, 103
Hegel, Georg, 3
hell, 88–89, 103
Hinduism. *See* models, Hindu stages of life
Hippocrates, 41
Hollis, James, xiv, xvi–xvii, 15–16, 95, 101
Holmes, Urban, 35–39
Holy Spirit, 54, 55, 61, 75, 131

Irenaeus (bishop), 42

Jesus Christ, 32, 54, 55, 56, 57, 59–60, 61–62, 66, 67, 70, 81, 82, 89, 90–92, 100, 125, 139, 140
  and prayer, 115
John of the Cross, xii, 71–72
Jung, Carl G., xiii, xv, 24, 30, 32, 39, 40, 77, 78, 80, 83, 104, 116

Kabbalah, 47
Keller, Helen, 100
Kierkegaard, Søren, 81
Kiersey, David, 43–46
Kingdom of God, xi, 89, 92, 113
Kohlberg, Lawrence, 12–13
Kretschmer, Ernst, 42

Lectio Divina, 58, 59, 130–33
Lesser, Elizabeth, xiv, 110
liminality, 77, 78
Loyal Soldier, xiii, 69–72, 82, 86, 87
Loyola, Ignatius, 59–60

Marx, Karl, 3
Mary Magdalene, 60–61
MBTI (Myers Briggs Type Indicator), 23–31, 43, 83
McLaren, Brian, 5, 88–89, 113, 118
meditation, 58, 110, 114, 122, 123, 131
Merton, Thomas, 107
midlife, xiii, 76–92
mind, 101, 102, 110, 116
mindfulness, x, 61, 87, 110, 111, 121

models, developmental
  Hindu stages of life, 5–6
  Hindu typology, 31–32
  John Wesley's "Trilateral" model, 6–7
  moral, 12–13
  psychological, 7–13, 15–20
  spiritual, 3–5, 13–15, 20–22, 23–50
Moore, Thomas, 101, 104, 106
Moses, xvi, 32, 113
Mother Teresa, 113
Muhammad, 32, 113
Muto, Susan, xiv, 113

Norberg, Tilda, 49, 78
Nouwen, Henri, 112

Palmer, Helen, 48
passion. *See* stamina
Passover, 58
Paul (apostle), 66, 67, 68, 71, 123, 131
Peck, M. Scott, 13, 15
Penfield, Wilder, 102
Perls, Fritz, 49, 78
personality type, 24–39
  temperament and, 40–46
  See also MBTI
Peter (apostle), 75, 125
physical body, 101–2, 109–10
Piaget, Jean, 10–12
Plato, 41–42, 47
Plotkin, Bill, xiv, xv, 16–20, 67, 69, 84–88
prayer(s), xvi, 52, 58, 60, 113, 114, 120, 129–33
  Jesus and, 115
  See also contemplative (centering) prayer; Lectio Divina
Pythagoras, 47

Richardson, Peter Tufts, 32–35
Ricoeur, Paul, 3, 95
rites of passage, 84–88
ritual(s), xvi, 56–58
Rohr, Richard, xii, xiv, xvi, 20–22, 62, 65, 71, 82, 85, 97, 98, 114, 123, 124

sacrament(s), xvi, 114
salvation, 73, 88, 89

Subject/Name Index

samtusta (non-craving), 111–12
scripture(s), 54–56, 58–60, 114, 131–33, 139–40
    journey motif in, 72–75
second half of life. *See* second journey
second journey, ix, x, xiii, xvi, xix, xx, 16, 65, 70–71, 75, 78, 79, 80, 81–82, 87, 95–100, 108–22, 124–25
    qualities of, 96–97, 97–98, 127–28
second simplicity. *See* second journey
Self, xviii, xviiin3, 16, 16n6, 21, 45, 77, 78, 83, 87, 88–89, 107
service, xiii, 72, 100, 108, 118–19, 122
shadow, the, 78
simplicity, xiii, 108, 111–12
sin, 89–90
skillful means, 120–21
Smith, Huston, 101–2, 110
solitude, 99, 112. *See also* stillness
soul, x, xi, xvi, xvii, xix, 77, 84–85, 101–7, 108, 114, 116, 118
soulcentric, 17, 20, 66, 84
soulfulness, xiii, 105, 108–9, 111
spirit, 85, 87, 101, 102
Spirit, 44, 102, 118
spiritual growth, 51–62
spirituality, xi, xxi, 52, 78, 86–87, 88, 104, 105, 106, 108, 109, 110, 117

and personality, xx, 23–24, 31–39, 49–50, 51, 52
and temperament, 40–46
and theology, 88–92
goal of, 114, 116
types of, 23–50
Spränger, Eduard, 42
stages of life/faith. *See* models
stamina, xiii, 108, 117–18
stillness, xiii, 108, 112–13. *See also* solitude
study, xiii, 108, 116–17
symbol, 57, 61

temperament, 40–46
Temple, William, 118–19
Ten Commandments, 67, 81
Teresa of Avila, 21
transcendence, xi, 104
Tree of Knowledge, 136–38, 139
Tree of Life, 136, 138, 139
truth, xxi, 106, 117
typology. *See* models

Wesley, John, 6–7
Westerhoff, John, 39
Wilber, Ken, 89, 118
worship, xvi, 118, 139

www.ingramcontent.com/pod-product-compliance
Lightning Source LLC
Chambersburg PA
CBHW071504150426
43191CB00009B/1409